Ichimoku Charts

Ichimoku Charts

An Introduction to
Ichimoku Kinko Clouds

Second Edition

Nicole Elliott

Hh

Hh Harriman House

HARRIMAN HOUSE LTD
18 College Street
Petersfield
Hampshire
GU31 4AD
GREAT BRITAIN
Tel: +44 (0)1730 233870
Email: enquiries@harriman-house.com
Website: www.harriman-house.com

First published in Great Britain in 2007
This second edition published 2018
Copyright © Nicole Elliott

Paperback ISBN: 978-0-85719-608-8
eBook ISBN: 978-0-85719-611-8

British Library Cataloguing in Publication Data
A CIP catalogue record for this book can be obtained from the British Library.

*Without Yuichiro Harada's help I would not
have got this far.*

Every owner of a physical copy of this edition of

Ichimoku Charts

can download the eBook for free direct from us at Harriman House,
in a format that can be read on any eReader, tablet or smartphone.

Simply head to:

ebooks.harriman-house.com/ichimokucharts2e

to get your free eBook now.

Contents

Preface to the Second Edition

Not that long ago, and out of the blue, my editor at Harriman House, contacted me about a new edition of my book. He said my book was still selling well, though it was first published ten years ago. How time flies when one is buried in work! But, yes, I thought, a re-fresh might be a good idea.

I asked what sort of thing he had in mind. He replied, "Start with the reviews on Amazon as that'll give you a clue as to areas that might need clarification or improvement." And then he added, "I must warn you, some of the reviews are very *robust*".

Thank goodness he had warned me because, after reading them, I wasn't sure whether to a) shoot myself, b) dismiss many of the writers as losers and pedants, or c) focus only on the nicest comments and try to create a rosy aura around myself. All three options were obviously unsatisfactory. Having toughened up in a trading pit, dealing room, and sales environment, I wasn't going to let them get me down. I decided to fight back.

This August I received a Friend Request on Facebook. It read:

> Hello! I hope you are the real Nicole Elliott. It is an honour if it is the case. Check my live Ichimoku trend scanner at: www.investdata.ooowebhostapp.com/alerts

I now know that his name is Didier Vally and he lives in Ozoir-La-Ferrière, France. He is one of the many people from all over the world who are fans of the Cloud charts. Do a quick search on Twitter and you'll soon get an idea of how popular the technique has become. I'm amazed and pleased that my ten-year-old book kicked off this worldwide interest. Widespread use has moved this method of analysis into the mainstream and is now part of the syllabus of the Diploma course run by the UK Society of Technical Analysts. Ichimoku charts now regularly appear in finance magazines and the business section of newspapers.

As for the moaners, I think they have three main themes. First, why buy the book when you can get this stuff for free on the internet? Second, it doesn't tell you how to trade with the Clouds. Finally, that there is either not enough depth or that some bits are irrelevant.

Let me remind you; when I started learning and using Cloud charts in 1997 there was *nothing* written on the subject in anything but Japanese (which I still cannot read). Zero, zilch, nada for me to go by. There I was, totally alone, feeling my way and scared of failing as a technical analyst in a Japanese environment surrounded by keen chartists.

After three years of learning from colleagues and using the method daily on foreign exchange, the chairman of the Society of Technical Analysts asked me at a meeting if I'd learnt anything from my experiences at the Industrial Bank of Japan. "Yes", I said, "Cloud charts". He immediately invited me to give a lecture on the subject for his members as he felt certain they'd be interested. Roping in a very nervous Japanese co-worker and teacher of Ichimoku, Harada-san, the lecture went down a storm with other market professionals. Likewise, at the London IFTA conference in 2002 when I devised option strategies using the Cloud charts because the theme of the conference was: 'Maximising profit potential'.

From there, Harriman House asked me to write a book on FX trading and I suggested Ichimoku Cloud charts instead; they loved the idea. We decided it was to be very much an introduction for Westerners to the method. The basics, as no one at that time had a clue about Ichimoku. And yes, I really did stick to the basics – *all* of them. Even today too many practitioners are not even aware of the Three Principles.

I asked my colleagues to order Sasaki's book from Japan. They laughed and asked why I would buy a book I couldn't read. Secretly, I think they were quite chuffed that I'd taken such a serious interest in something totally Japanese. Years later I did enquire as to how much it would cost to do a reprint of Goichi Hosoda's original text which had been out of print for decades. The family, who guard his reputation fiercely, suggested US$30,000. I, and I think others, have left it at that.

My book was never intended as a 'teach yourself how to trade' handbook; there are more than enough of those sort of things peddled by snake-oil salesmen. I am a trader first and foremost, a corporate banker through and through, and now a financial journalist with the Financial Times Group and the *South China Morning Post*. I'm not here to spoon-feed lazy people who believe they can get rich quick. I think that if one doesn't put in the effort to really grasp the subject, Clouds or anything else for that matter, one can never be really confident. It limits one's ability to question, to turn the subject on its head and see if it's still fit for purpose. The book was intended to give readers, admittedly aiming more at market professionals, enough information to do their own research and decide whether to incorporate the method or not. It's a primer for the novice to Ichimoku – which, in 2007, included just about anyone who could not speak Japanese.

As to whether there is enough depth, that is in the eye of the beholder. My book should give you the basics and then it's up to you to put them into practice in any way you see fit – if at all. Some reader comments are quite frankly wrong: like the one about the wave method being a rehash and not part of Ichimoku charts. Wrong, completely wrong. Wave, Price, and Timespan are absolutely integral to the principle of Clouds. Time and price are inextricably linked as another reader spotted, saying Chapter 4 was the most important and useful.

If the writing style is considered flippant, dry, sardonic and light, this does not mean that the content is too. On the contrary, most writers consider it a badge of honour to make a book easy to read, easy on the eye, and mercifully concise. Plodding, turgid text is best kept to scientific research papers.

As to the nice comments, I cannot thank those who wrote them enough. Deeply, from my heart; all of us need some encouragement along the way and a helping hand at times. And they say that people who are nice to others are also nearly always happier than the fiercely critical. Or, as linguist Zhou Youguang who died very recently at the age of 111 said, "when you encounter difficulties, you need to be optimistic. The pessimists tend to die". One to remember.

Finally, when I wrote the book in 2006 (finishing it off in winter at a mountain resort in Switzerland, because I don't ski), though I had plenty of trading experience – and even more in technical analysis – I had never written a book; I had not even thought of doing so. I cannot tell you how delighted I was when, at the IFTA conference in Paris in 2008, a veteran analyst came to me after I'd made my presentation and said, "Nicole, you speak exactly as you write. I've read your book and enjoyed it. Well done." One must try to be true to one's voice and style.

Now, with another decade of daily use under my belt, I give you further musings on the method, and how I've adapted bits of it to suit my needs. My honest thoughts are: a) you are lucky that an investment banker with 15 years' experience under her belt had the pluck to delve into a totally unknown area of technical analysis – and maybe get it all wrong. That b) my publisher took on the risk of printing a book on a completely unknown subject. And now c) that Cloud charting is considered mainstream, not just in technical analysis circles but media where, for example, the *South China Morning Post* in Hong Kong publishes Cloud charts of mine several times a week. That it is taught at Diploma level was, in large part, down to Stephen Eckett of Harriman House. With thanks.

Preface

Who this book is for

The book has been written for existing users of candlestick charts who want to extend their knowledge and techniques to include Ichimoku Cloud charts. As such, some knowledge of technical analysis is assumed, especially a knowledge of candlesticks (although a brief primer on candlesticks is also included in the book's appendix).

What this book covers

The book covers the history of candlestick charts - explaining the context in which they developed. It then moves on to explain how in the 1940s and 1950s a journalist, with the pseudonym Ichimoku Sanjin, started refining candlestick analysis by adding a series of moving averages. The book explains in detail how to construct Cloud charts and how to interpret them. A chapter is devoted to the advanced analysis of Cloud charts, with an in-depth study of the Three Principles: Wave Principle, price target and Timespan Principle. The book is illustrated throughout with numerous examples of Cloud chart analysis.

How the book is structured

The book comprises eight main chapters:

1. History

A brief history of candlesticks and the development of Ichimoku Kinko Hyo.

2. Constructing the Cloud Charts

First, a quick introduction to candlestick charts – the foundation of Ichimoku – and then a detailed explanation of how Ichimoku charts are constructed.

3. Interpretation of the Clouds

How to interpret the Cloud charts, including: identifying support and resistance levels; the significance of Cloud thickness and the distance between price and Cloud; and how to finesse trading positions.

4. The Three Principles

A discussion of the three principles of Ichimoku charts: the Wave Principle, price targets and the Timespan Principle.

5. Case Studies

Several case studies are included that work through in detail the interpretation of Ichimoku chart examples.

6. Option Trading with Clouds

How the unique combination of timing and price levels that is possible with Ichimoku analysis is particularly relevant for option trading strategies.

7. An Update on How I Use Cloud Charts Today

An overview on how my use of Cloud charts has evolved since the first edition of this book was published ten years ago.

8. New Case Study

An example of how I analyse charts today. We work through a series of daily and weekly charts without knowing what the underlying market is.

Introduction

A LONG TIME ago, and more years than I would care to admit to, I started my first City job as a junior dealer at the then small Bank of Scotland. Working in the money market section, with what at that time were cutting-edge interest rate futures, my two bosses (there were only three of us) said:

> You will be our expert on charts. All the futures dealers in Chicago use these, so off you go and learn.

And so I did. Later, armed with a pencil, graph paper, a couple of brief lessons under my belt and bare-faced cheek, I wormed my way in to the offices of the few jobbers and brokers who knew about technical analysis.

I immediately knew I had found my niche, and still today I often think my job is such fun. Everyday I have a jigsaw puzzle where I have all of the pieces, but there is no image to fit them to. You have to work the big picture out by yourself. It is also a little like dancing. Sometimes it is pure hard slog: tiring, tedious, repetitive, constant discipline, and my partner has two left feet. Then the other times (which more than make up for everything else) it's truly fantastic, intuitive, creative, and I have Fred Astaire to lead me round the dance floor.

Over the years the pencil and paper were replaced with computer programs. Then one day I noticed a new technical study had been added to the vast array I already had to choose from. Called Ichimoku Kinko Hyo, I had never heard of it, despite having practised as a full-time Technical Analyst for almost twenty years. My initial reaction was one of shock-horror, when I looked at a chart and saw something that looked like a writhing mass of knotted, multicoloured noodles.

I left the noodles alone for a while; but then ten years ago I went to work for a Japanese bank, and recognised the charts many of my Japanese colleagues were using: Spaghetti Junction! Curiosity got the better of me and – at the risk of losing my street cred as sole full-time chartist in a very macho dealing room – I asked them what these were.

"Oh, Cloud charts," they said. "We all use them." They did, and still do. And now I do too.

When the markets were quiet, I asked our very busy dollar/yen dealer, Harada-san, if he could explain them to me. Slowly (as he was very busy), and despite some language problems, I began to understand. Setting them up on my files, I started to use them every day. Questions arose as I went along, which then allowed me to progress to the next level with his explanations.

I now realise how much I owe Harada-san, because all the books on the subject are in Japanese and, quite frankly, I am too old to start learning a language in order to learn a new charting method.

This book distils what I've learnt about Ichimoku Kinko Hyo over the last few years of working in a Japanese dealing room. I like the method and now use it every day – because it works. I hope you too find the Clouds fascinating and profitable.

1

HISTORY

IN THIS SHORT chapter I thought it would be interesting to briefly describe the political and economic background that prevailed at the time that candlesticks were first thought of, and how Ichimoku Cloud charts evolved from these. The chapter ends with a calligraphic diversion that analyses the Chinese characters for Ichimoku Kinko Hyo.

Edo, candlesticks and Ichimoku Kinko Hyo

Political and economic background

The use of charting increased as Japan emerged from a feudal period of constant war, where the emperor in Kyoto and his military deputy, the shogun, had lost all control (1500 to 1600). A process of unification began, known as the Edo period, which lasted from 1600 until the Meiji Restoration in 1868. During this time, Japan was cut off from the outside world and developed a highly individual society and set of values. Missionaries were expelled in 1587, and in 1633 a decree was passed prohibiting Japanese from trading with foreigners or living abroad. These measures reinforced the power of central government. Many see this as a time when every aspect of life was uniquely Japanese.

One of the generals responsible for restoring order in Japan at the beginning of the Edo period was Tokugawa Ieyasu. He took the title of shogun in 1603 and his family went on to rule until 1868. He governed from Edo (now called Tokyo) and his government, known as the bakufu, administered his lands. The bakufu oversaw the samurai officials, who in turn were responsible for collecting taxes and maintaining order. He realised that the key to holding on to power was separating out roles and legitimising landholdings in order to assess crop yields.

The nobility were isolated from politics in Kyoto and had little contact with the outside world, devoting themselves to scholarship, classical culture and religion. Far-flung provinces were allowed to keep their feudal lords, the daimyo. To keep a close eye on the daimyo they were expected to spend half the year in Edo, at their own considerable expense – swelling the population of the city to one million by 1700 and making it one of the largest cities in the world.

After careful surveys all land was recorded and assessed for crop yields. This was the basis of taxation and was measured as to how many koku of rice it would yield (one koku being about five bushels). Peasants paid 40% to the governing bodies, usually in rice but later also in cash. Their weapons had been confiscated in 1588, so their role was completely different from that of the samurais. Land under cultivation doubled in this period and yields increased significantly with better tools and the pooling of resources. Clustering around castles, craftsmen and merchants supplied the goods and services needed by peasants, warriors and government officials. Known as chonin, meaning townspeople, they formed the basis of an increasingly important class and were what we would call merchants.

The bakufu supervised land routes, primarily for military purposes, but these were not especially suitable for transporting goods. Sea routes and rivers were successfully adopted as an alternative, the route between the northeast and Osaka being especially busy as it linked the major cities. Increased stability also meant that local markets declined in importance as centralized government gained control. Trade between regions grew steadily with Osaka dominating finance and commerce. It had large warehouses in which raw materials were stored, which in turn allowed for the stabilization of the prices of goods.

The Dojima Rice Exchange, set up in the late 1600s, was the first of its kind and by 1710 was trading in warehouse receipts as well as the physical commodity. Rice coupons, a precursor to futures contracts, could be re-sold and when the coinage became debased were the most accepted and useful medium of exchange.

At about this time the merchants became especially powerful because the samurai and lords were deeply indebted to them. Luxurious city living and long periods away from home had taken their toll. By 1800, merchants were able to marry into the feudal and political classes (which previously had been prohibited), resulting in them wielding greater political power.

In this climate of change, villages in the country began to suffer from peasant revolts, because of the deteriorating economic situation and as a protest against the class divide. Inflation was a persistent problem, exacerbating difficult policy choices, so that in 1859 the bakufu were forced to open up ports to foreigners. A few years later, in 1868, Tokugawa power ended and imperial rule was restored.

Candlesticks

The man widely credited with perfecting candlesticks, and making a fortune in the process, was Munehisa Homma (1724-1803), who lived in the Edo period described above. Nicknamed 'Sakata', because he first worked at Shonai Sakata - a commercial town in northern Japan - he was the youngest son who, unusually, took over the family trading business, before moving to Edo (Tokyo).

Sakata postulated five rules for successful trading. Using carefully chosen alliterative words, he used the prefix of 'san' meaning three, which for the Japanese is a sort of 'magical' number (like lucky 7 or unlucky 13 to some Westerners). The number three is believed to mark the start or turning point of a series of events. Sakata's five rules are:

1. Sanzan – three mountains,

2. Sanpei – three soldiers,

3. Sansen – three rivers,

4. Sankoo – three spaces, and

5. Sanpo – three laws.

Using these rules he aimed and managed to separate out 'value' from the 'price' of rice contracts – the fear and the greed of his counterparties, supply and demand. Using his methods, Sakata was rumoured to have had the longest ever winning streak of 100 consecutive profitable trades.

Some say that because of all the upheaval during its evolution, and the dominant role of the army, many candlestick patterns have military connotations. However, 'three white/black soldiers' is the only one that immediately springs to my mind. Many of the others are just as likely to be linked with stars, animals or people. Some, like 'Doji' (which means 'simultaneously'), convey whether buyers or sellers are the dominant force (neither in the case of a Doji candlestick).

We can note, in passing, that the evolution in Japan of price charts in the 17th century, and candlesticks in the 18th century, easily pre-dates the first American bar charts of the 1880s.

Ichimoku Kinko – a refinement of candlesticks

Moving swiftly on to just before the outbreak of World War II, a journalist called Goichi Hosoda started adapting and refining candlestick analysis by adding a series of moving averages. He used the pseudonym 'Ichimoku Sanjin', where the first Chinese character of his name means 'at a glance'. The other characters mean 'of a man standing on a mountain', harking back to Homma's three mountains, but also to give a sense of the perspective and clarity this type of charting brings. Starting in the 1940s he analysed share prices and eventually published a book outlining his method in 1968 – after forcing many students to crunch thousands of numbers for him. This was, of course, before the advent of affordable computers, so it was a very laborious process. I believe that the use of pseudonyms has been common in Japan for a great many years. Perhaps this is why my esteemed colleague, Harada-san, was happy with his nickname 'Richie' (as in Richie Rich with the glasses). The famous artist Hokusai changed his pseudonym up to 36 times, possibly each time he changed the style of his work but maybe just to match his mood.

More recently, the method was revived by Hidenobu Sasaki of Nikko Citigroup Securities, who published Ichimoku Kinko Studies in 1996. Now in its 18th edition, this is the book most Japanese use, and has been voted the best technical analysis book in the Nikkei newspaper for nine consecutive years.

Be aware that candlesticks are not the only charts used in Japan. As well as acknowledging Western methods, my Japanese colleagues are equally happy using Renko, Three-Line-Break charts and Kagi charts. As many charting packages do not offer these, they are religiously drawn by hand every day. This is really for purists and those who only follow one or two main instruments. Being so laborious it does not lend itself to cross-market analysis. However, walk into any Japanese dealing room today and the most common charts you'll see will be Ichimoku Kinko Clouds.

Calligraphy

The Chinese character for 'bar charts'

comes from the word 'foot', alluding to the idea that markets leave footprints, which can then be followed, read and interpreted.

In Japan three alphabets are used for writing. Kanji, the most ancient script, was introduced in the 5th century from China via Korea. In kanji each little pattern sums up an entire concept and corresponds to a word. Hence, the patterns are ideograms and are what are known as 'Chinese characters'.

Two other scripts were developed in 9th-century Japan and are the first truly Japanese writing. They are phonetic and have 46 syllables of which 5 are vowels. Hiragana is more cursive, while Katakana is more angular and mainly used for foreign words.

All three scripts are either written across the page from left to right, or vertically from top to bottom and right to left. Japanese newspapers are read 'back to front'.

Back to the Chinese character for 'bar chart', known as 'Hyo'. Look at this next set of characters:

一目均衡表

Once again you can see the kanji for 'chart' at the end on the right. The one on the far left, that looks like a minus sign, is pronounced 'ichi' and means one or ace. The second character, that looks like a ladder, is 'moku', which means look, sight or eye. In fact it is a drawing of an upended, stylised eyeball – which is really very appropriate. The middle character is 'kin' meaning equal or even, and the fourth is 'ko' or 'kou', in Western pronunciation, and means even, scale or bar; think of it as balance.

Putting this all together you can read it as 'one eye equal scale chart'. But when pulling the words together there are subtle changes to the meaning of the whole, just as adjectives nuance the tone of objects, or as adverbs do to verbs. Therefore walk and smart actually means walking with poise and purpose and is the way one moves through Ichimoku. Thus you end up with a phrase that is read as 'at a glance balanced chart'.

Terminology

The correct name of these charts is: Ichimoku Kinko Hyo. But this is something of a mouthful, so the charts are often referred to as Ichimoku charts or Cloud charts. Occasionally one might come across Ichimoku Kinko Clouds, which again is the same thing. All these terms are used interchangeably in this book.

2

Constructing the Cloud Charts

Candlesticks – the foundation

THE FIRST THING to plot on your graph are candlesticks. If you're already familiar with candlesticks, then you might like to skip this section. (There's a brief primer on candlesticks in the Appendix.)

Candlesticks are similar to Western bar charts: the highest price of the period is plotted, the lowest, the opening price and the close for that period.

While bar charts have tiny little horizontal marks either side of the vertical bar to denote the open and close (and sometimes just the close), candles make the most of these two pieces of data. They are drawn as a fat bit either side of the bar and known as the real body. So, you have a thin vertical line joining the high and the low. Either side of this you have a fatter column joining the opening and the closing prices. This column is coloured (black or any other colour you choose) if the market closes lower than it opened, or left blank if it closes higher.

With the candles we watch for reversal patterns, which I find are usually much clearer than those on bar charts. Some of these have lovely names too, like Shooting or Evening Star, Three Black Crows, Spinning Top and Fry Pan Bottom, Abandoned Baby, and my favourite, Hanging Man!

It is only a small step from bars to candlesticks, but the difference is dramatic. Having started and worked with bar charts, the moment I switched to candles I wished I had done it years earlier as I was able to see the key points and interpret market action so much more quickly. This is very important to me because every morning I have to look at hundreds of charts and speed is of the essence.

(See diagrams below and the Appendix for candlestick patterns.)

A day in the life of a candle

Assume the instrument you are studying started the day at 100.00, the same price as it closed the previous evening. The candle would look as follows:

Just a small horizontal line:

███████████

Throughout the morning the market rallied to 105.00, therefore the candle would now look like this:

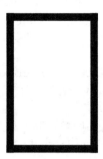

After lunch prices declined back down to where they had started, giving up all the morning's gains, and our candle would now look like this:

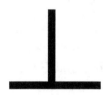

I think you will agree that the message is now very different (a 'Gravestone Doji') to what it had been when we happily skipped off to get some food.

Note that some civilized markets, like the Tokyo Stock Exchange, still stop for lunch. Some analysts plot the am and pm sessions separately making for two candles per day's worth of price action. This of course creates mayhem with moving averages and other oscillators, but it is then easy to look back on each block. I also use intraday candles for certain instruments and time horizons. I often use four-hourly ones as they keep the detail of how the market developed over the day without clogging up the screen with too much sideways work.

The following day our market may gap lower to 95.00, so our candles now look like so:

Then steadily and slowly throughout the whole of the next day prices climb and close at 105.00, making the two-day combination end like this:

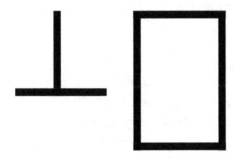

Not nearly as bearish now.

What I am trying to stress here is that only at the close of the day/period can we be confident whether we have formed an important chart pattern or whether it has all been noise, even if price action is fairly extreme. This may be obvious at the moment, but I urge you to remember this when working with weekly and monthly candles. It is so easy to focus on the very latest price action, forgetting that it all may come unravelled by the close.

Creating Ichimoku charts

Daily data and mid prices

Daily data is the standard frequency

Although traditional candle theory looks at hourly, daily, weekly or monthly charts, just as we do with bar charts, with Ichimoku charts only daily charts are used. Having said that, some chartists bend the rules and use monthly, weekly or hourly units of time – the lesson being: never be afraid to experiment.

The fact that daily candlesticks are used means that the system is for medium- to long-term strategies, and is therefore not suitable for jobbers and day traders.

Mid-point prices used

We now start moving into new territory! Ichimoku charts differ from Western ones in that they are not drawn using daily closing prices. Instead, 'mid-prices' are used. This method takes the average of the high and low price of the day (simply adding the high and low price and dividing by two). The mid-price calculation is not adjusted for volume.

This is a good method for markets where there is an arbitrary cut-off time, such as FX which is a global 24-hour market, or for small markets that are subject to manipulation at settlement time.

Moving averages

Candlesticks with moving averages

Once the daily candles are drawn, the next thing to do is add two moving averages. These are used in the same way as we do in the West, with crossovers giving buy or sell signals. When the short-term average is above the longer term one, the trend is to higher prices; when the short-term average drops below the longer one, that is a sell signal. A position is held until these reverse.

Figure 2-1: FTSE 100 with moving averages

Chart comment

Based purely on moving average crossovers, one would currently be long since early November.

For Ichimoku charts we use two specific moving averages which are:

1. **Tenkan-sen** ("Conversion Line"): is a *nine-day moving average*, and

2. **Kijun-sen** ("Base Line"): is a *twenty six-day moving average*.

As usual, the shorter moving average whips around the longer one, giving points at which positions should be switched from long to short and vice-versa.

The origins of 9 and 26 days as the moving average periods

The number of days used are related to the fact that in Japan they used to work a six-day week, Monday to Saturday, so that there is an average of 26 working days in a typical month. This period became the standard moving average. While, by trial and error, and exhaustive manual back-testing, nine days was found to give the best results when used in conjunction with 26 days. I feel sorry for the students who did all the legwork (pre-computers); and I believe they had to sign confidentiality agreements when working on this tedious task.

Should Western moving average periods be used?

It is often asked whether we should change the number of days used for the averages to reflect a five-day working week. Yes, maybe – in which case we would get the more conventional Western ten and twenty day ones.

The reason I have not done so is that the majority still stick to the industry standard. As my interest in all things charting is knowing where and when others will be forced to react – the psychology of the market – I want to be looking at the same things as they are.

So I stick with market conventions here as I do in all other aspects of technical analysis. With Western moving averages I stick to 10, 20, 50 and 200-day ones. In other words, I want to know where others will panic and flip, not where I will do so, because only then will important reversals occur. Remember: don't try and be too clever; just do what you do well because that's more than enough.

Moving averages as support and resistance levels

Another difference between Western methods and this one is that the averages, as well as telling you what trend you are in, are also in themselves support and resistance levels.

For example, in a bull market (*koten* in Japanese) prices may stall and consolidate on the way up. How far they are likely to pull back will depend on, among other things, where the averages lie.

The nine day average should usually be the line closest to current price, and will therefore be the first area of support limiting the pull-back. The 26-day moving average should be further from current price levels, and is a more important area of support. Prices often haul themselves up from here in bull markets but, if they don't, this is the first warning signal of a potential turn in trend.

In a bear market (*gyakuten* in Japanese) the same rules hold.

Figure 2-2: LME three-month copper with two moving averages

Chart comment

A very steady bull market where one would have held a long position since mid-September.

The degree of slope reflects the strength of the trend

Note also that the slope of the 26-day average is also fairly important. The steeper it is in a downtrend or an uptrend, the more powerful the current trend and the more likely it is to continue. However, if it is moving very gently lower/ higher, and especially if it is flat, then one assumes that there is no overall trend. An angle of between 33 and 45 degrees is great. This is regardless of moving average crossovers. For example, see EUR/GBP in the next chart.

Figure 2-3: Euro/sterling with two moving averages

Chart comment

Swinging randomly one penny either side of £0.6820.

As you can see in the chart above, this method really does not work for markets that are not trending. The green line is the 26-day moving average which has been pretty much flat-lining since September. Ichimoku charts are therefore very much a trend-following system.

Looking ahead

As well as for the averages nine and 26 days ahead are also used as potential stalling points within a larger move. Assuming an important high was formed on today's chart, Japanese traders will pinpoint nine and 26 working days ahead, and watch these dates for signs that a smaller wave within one of a larger degree has ended.

For some reason they also sometimes use eighteen days (which is not 26-9). [This is discussed in detail in a later chapter.]

Figure 2-4: Spot gold with projections for 9, 18, and 26 days ahead from an important low

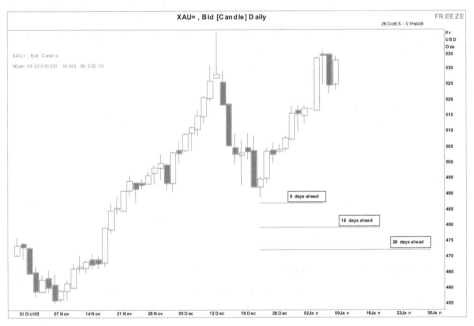

This concept may be familiar for those of you who use Cycle Theory. This method again starts with an important high or low, and projects forward in time Fibonacci numbers' worth of days. Where a series of cycles meet on a particular day in the future, there is a greater chance of forming important highs or lows.

Drawing the Cloud

After plotting candles and averages, the next step is to plot the two lines that form the actual Cloud.

Refer to Figure 2-5 to understand the explanation that follows.

Figure 2-5: FTSE 100 with moving averages and Clouds

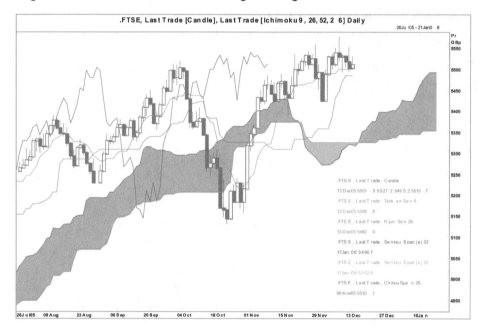

The daily candles are here, in blue as we saw them before. The moving averages are calculated: pink for the 9 day and dark green for the 26 day.

Senkou Span A and B

1. The **first line** of the Cloud, the deep pink one, is known as Senkou Span A ('Leading Span A') and is calculated by adding the Tenkan (9-day average) and Kijun (26-day average) values and dividing by two. This line is then plotted 26 days ahead of the last complete day's trading.

2. The **second line** (turquoise), imaginatively called Senkou Span B ('Leading Span B'), is calculated by finding the highest price of the last 52 days, adding

to it the lowest price of the last 52 days, and dividing by two. This is also plotted 26 days ahead.

So, although the two lines have similar names, their construction is very different. The space between these two lines is shaded – *that is the Cloud.*

Note

Some programs change the colour of the Cloud depending on whether Span A or Span B is on top – as in the charts provided here by Reuters. The shading alternates between the deep pink if Span A is on top and turquoise if Span B is on top. While not exactly incorrect, it is irrelevant.

Senkou Span A

Senkou Span A is like a weighted average of the last 26 days, being the sum of the 9-day and the 26-day moving averages divided by two.

Senkou Span B

Senkou Span B is similar to a 50% retracement level and is the mid-point of the last 52 days. Span B is often flat because extra weight is given to important highs and lows; these levels remaining in the calculation until either a new high or low is posted. Otherwise 52 days have to elapse for the level of the Cloud to change. The idea is of time marching on with support and resistance remaining constant at the 50% level during consolidation periods.

Two halves of the market, plus time, lies at the core of the Ichimoku Kinko charting.

Another example of the Senkou Spans A and B, with coloured Cloud in between, can be seen in the CAD/SGD chart below.

Figure 2-6: Singapore dollars per Canadian dollar with Senkou Spans A and B

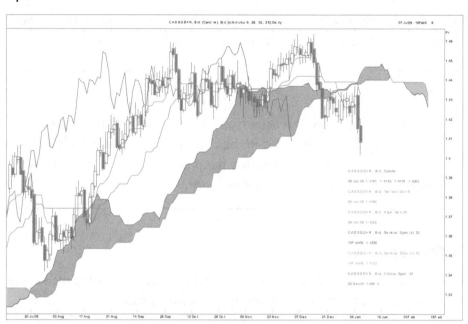

Chart comment

Note how fat the Cloud is early November and how thin it becomes mid-December.

Similar to trend lines

Many find the idea of plotting some sort of average price ahead of time extraordinary. But if you think of these lines not as averages, but as some sort of a trend, you will see that in the West we often plot lines out into the future. Trend lines, of course, but also the lines that limit formations like triangles, the neckline of a head-and-shoulder top, broadening tops, and Gann fan lines too.

And that's it, as far as constructing the Clouds goes. In the next chapter we'll look at how to interpret the Clouds.

Chikou Span

The final line to be added is Chikou Span ('Lagging Span').

Figure 2-7: Yen per US dollar with Chikou Span

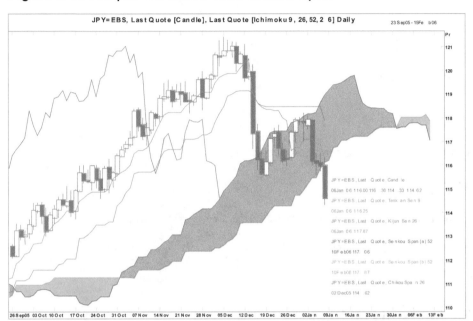

Note

Some chart packages plot the current price 25 days back. You will know whether this is the case as the lines bob up and down during the day as the current price changes.

In the above chart, Chikou Span can be seen as the dark green line. This is today's closing price plotted 26 days behind the last daily close.

Example – calculations for Ichimoku construction

Data

On 10 October 2005 the price data for the FTSE 100 was:

High   5,395.8

Low   5,362.3

Close 5,374.5

Calculations

On this day (10 October 2005) we can calculate:

Mid-price

Mid-price = (high price + low price)/2

$\quad\quad$ = (5,395.8+5,362.3)/2

$\quad\quad$ = 5,379.1

Tenkan-sen and Kijun-sen

Tenkan-sen = 5,448.3 (9 day moving average)

Kijun-sen = 5,404.4 (26 day moving average)

Senkou Span A

Senkou Span A = (Tenkan-sen + Kijun-sen)

$\quad\quad$ = (5,448.3 + 5,404.4)/2

$\quad\quad$ = 5,426.3

Senkou Span B

Highest high (previous 52 days) = 5,515.0

Lowest low (previous 52 days)   = 5,228.1

Senkou Span B = (Highest High + Lowest Low)/2

= (5,515.0 + 5,228.1)/2

= 5,204.3

Chikou Span

Chikou Span = closing price

= 5,374.5

Plotting

With the data calculated above we can then plot the following points on the chart:

5 Sep 05 (10 Oct 05 – 26 days)

We plot:

Chikou Span = 5,374.5

10 Oct 05

We plot:

Tenkan-sen = 5,448.3

Kijun-sen = 5,404.4

15 Nov 05 (10 Oct 05 + 26 days)

We plot:

Senkou Span A = 5,300.2

Senkou Span B = 5,204.3

A table of Ichimoku calculations for the FTSE 100 around this period can be found in the Appendix.

Summary

Ichimoku charts are built around candlestick charts with the following five lines added:

1. **Tenkan-sen** (Highest High + Lowest Low)/2, for the past 9 periods
2. **Kijun-sen** (Highest High + Lowest Low)/2, for the past 26 periods
3. **Senkou Span A** (Tenkan-Sen + Kijun-Sen)/2, plotted 26 periods ahead
4. **Senkou Span B** (Highest High + Lowest Low)/2, for the past 52 periods, plotted 26 periods ahead
5. **Chikou Span** Today's closing price plotted 26 periods behind

---

Note

Mid-prices are used for all lines except Chikou Span.

The three key **time periods** are 9, 26, 52.

The **Cloud** is the area between Senkou Span A and Senkou Span B.

3

Interpretation of the Clouds

THE CLOUDS HAVE a variety of uses and add a completely new dimension to the standard candlestick chart.

Support/resistance levels

Firstly, if today's candle is above the Cloud, the trend is for higher prices. The top of the Cloud is the first level of support and the bottom is the second level of support.

From experience, I have seen that these really do often work, but one has to give them a little leeway. Normally, I would also wait until the end of the day to see whether the closing price is below the Cloud, before even beginning to consider whether the trend has reversed.

The opposite is the case when candles are below the Cloud, with this becoming the area of resistance.

Often the market seems to move through the first support/resistance level and fails somewhere in the middle of the Cloud. When this happens we watch the shape of daily candlesticks to see if they give a reversal signal.

Figure 3-1: CBOT front month corn futures contract with Clouds

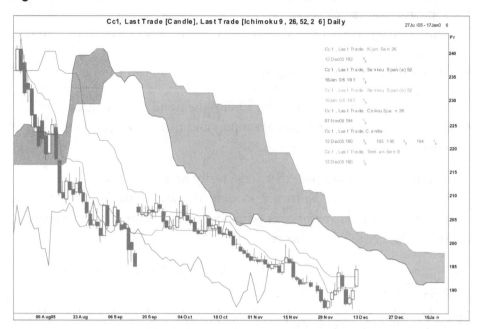

Chart comment

Note the stepped Senkou Span B line, as slowly the high of the last 52 days drops out.

Finessing trading positions

Clouds can be very useful in adjusting a basic trading position. Partial profits can be taken or tentative new positions can be entered into without waiting for the moving averages to cross. (See Chapter 6, 'Options Trading with Clouds', for more details.)

Cloud thickness

The thickness of the Cloud is important. The thicker the Cloud, the less likely it is that prices will manage a sustained break through it. The thinner the Cloud, and a break through has a much better chance.

So, Cloud is Cloud regardless of whether Span A or Span B is on top; the thickness is what matters.

Crossover points

I have often been asked whether the crossover point of the Senkou Spans is important. No, other than the fact that at that point the Cloud is at its thinnest.

Figure 3-2: Cable (US dollars per pound sterling) with Clouds

Chart comment

Senkou Span B is often a horizontal, as important highs/lows remain in place for a long time.

Trend reversals

Thin sections in the Cloud give us an idea of when the market is likely to change trend. Look ahead and see when, and at what price, it gets very thin.

Similarly, if the Cloud is getting fatter and fatter, the chance of a reversal in trend lessens looking out into the future. It gives dates (I'd say three or four days around the central day) when there is an increased chance of a successful move through the Cloud area.

Also indicated are price levels that need to be broken for a significant turn, with the move accelerating as prices slice though the crossover point.

Distance between price and Cloud

The distance between the Cloud and the current price is not significant.

Again, Western methods often suggest that when prices are a long way from a trend line, or two averages, the market is unstable and possibly out of control. Not so with this method.

In some ways it is a similar idea to that of the 26-day moving average which, when very steep, means a powerful trend in place. As a concept, it is the opposite of the Relative Strength Index, or reversion to the mean.

However, when faced with soar-away price-action, I watch far more closely for reversal candlesticks. It does feel churlish to warn that 'the end is nigh' when others are rushing in to buy, and we all know not to count our chickens before they hatch. And powerful moves can be short-lived but take prices way beyond what anyone had hoped for. But it cannot last forever, so watch for signs of instability in the candlesticks themselves.

Figure 3-3: Spot gold with Clouds

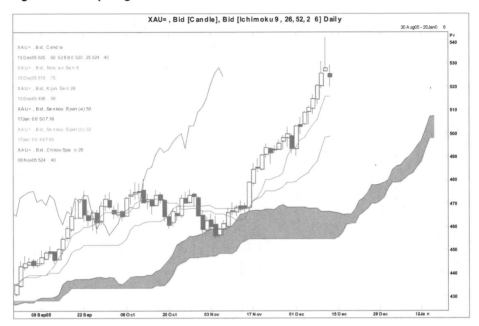

Chart comment

This major market is up 25% in just one month – probably difficult to sustain. Note also the massive Shooting Star candle on 12 December; certainly warning of instability.

Clouds are for trending markets

Remember, this is a system for *markets that are trending*. In sideways markets it is hopeless, as you can see in the first two thirds of the chart below of the S&P 500.

Figure 3-4: S&P 500 index with Clouds

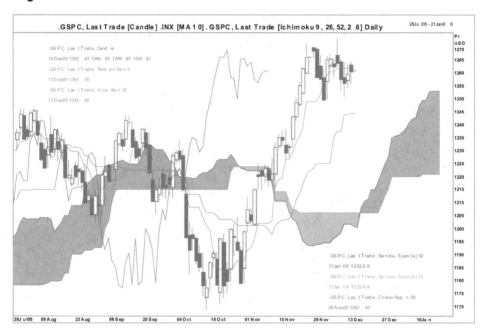

Chart comment

Moving broadly sideways from July to November so the Clouds are of no use.

Chikou Span

We'll look again at the chart we saw a little earlier.

Figure 3-5: Yen per US dollar with Chikou Span

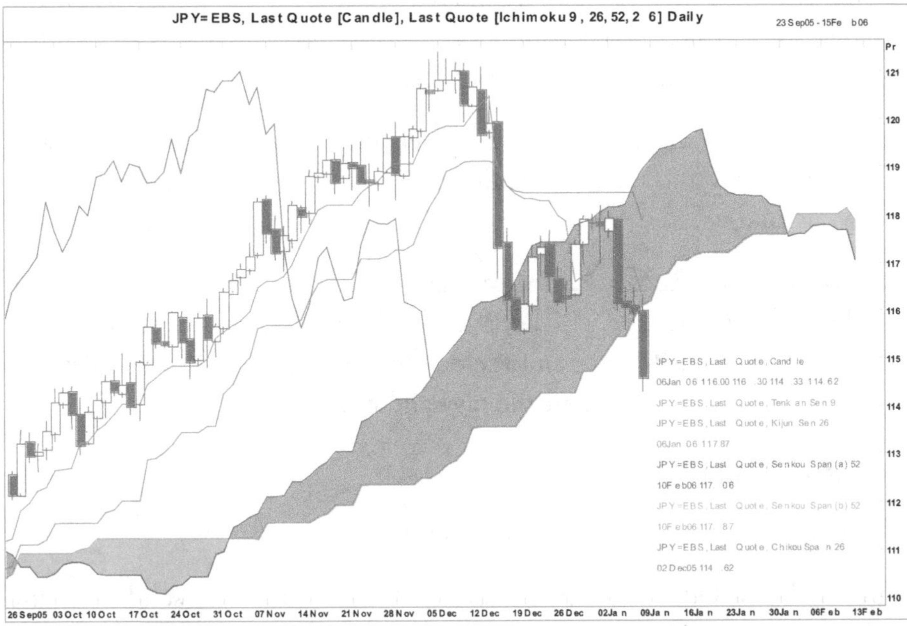

Chart comment

Note how quickly Chikou Span (dark green line) drops to the Cloud in December, then clings within the Cloud's upper and lower boundaries.

Chikou Span is used in combination with *today's* candlestick:

- if Chikou Span is trading above the candlestick of 26 days ago, then today's market is said to be in a **bullish** long-term phase; conversely,
- if Chikou Span is trading below the candlestick of 26 days ago, then today's market is in a long-term **bearish** phase.

37

Same idea for Chikou Span itself and the Clouds: above the Cloud of 26 days ago, then today is bullish - and vice versa.

Support and resistance for Chikou Span

Finally, the position of the candlesticks themselves, the moving averages, and the Clouds are also levels of support and resistance for *Chikou Span*. These will give suggestions where today's support and resistance lie. The 9 and 26 day moving averages also act as support and resistance for Chikou Span.

It is a good idea to make a list of these levels first thing in the morning, as it can be quite fiddly and time consuming to have to keep checking back on the levels while trading.

Note that problems can arise if the candles around Chikou Span are very tall. It can be difficult to decide whether a level has been broken decisively. In this case I would wait until the end of the day to see whether the closing level of the line is clearly above or below the big candlesticks.

Interpretation summary

Try to visualize the whole analysis as follows:

- in a **bull market** Chikou Span and the Clouds provide a solid base, and above you is nothing but clear blue skies which will not hamper your way up; conversely,
- in a **bear market**, Chikou Span and dark heavy Clouds will grind you down and push you lower.

Figure 3-6: LME three-month forward Copper with Clouds and Chikou Span

Chart comment

Very steady and strong bull trend despite rather thin Clouds. No resistance whatsoever.

Figure 3-7: CME Eurodollar interest rate future with Clouds and Chikou Span

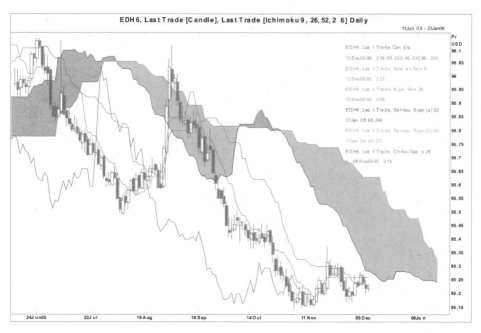

Chart comment

Heavy Clouds are grinding prices lower.

So you see the Clouds which are plotted ahead of time, coupled with today's price that is plotted behind time, are the really innovative elements that differentiate this type of charting from conventional Western analysis.

We shall now work through two charts in detail so you can understand the exact steps to take.

Example 1: Dax Index

The first example we will look at will be the German Dax stock market index.

Dax Index

You will see that the chart below contains many gaps, because, unlike the FTSE 100 and DJIA indices, the Dax can (and will often) open away from the previous day's close. The other two indices always open at the same price as the last close and will move up or down as bargains are struck in the different shares that make up the indices. Therefore we will not pay too much attention to these gaps in our analysis, only taking note of these when especially large gaps form, or when they are to be found around very important chart levels and patterns.

Figure 3.8: German Dax 30 Index

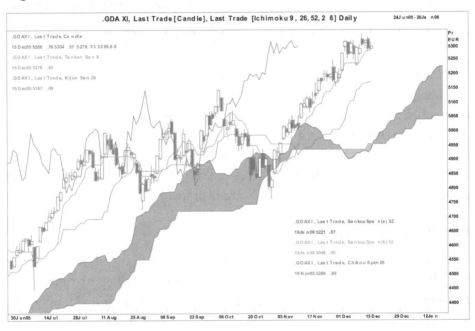

Chart comment

In an uptrend with consolidation late July to October.

Analysis

As can be seen from the above chart, prices had been moving steadily higher since November, after moving broadly sideways from late July to 28 October. Kijun-sen (the 26-day MA) tended to be horizontal then, but after the 28th started moving higher at an angle just over 45 degrees – similar to what it had been doing in July. The long-term bull trend which started in March 2003 has resumed.

So this is very much a go-stop-go sort of chart pattern, and is useful to learn how Ichimoku analysis performs under different conditions.

Tenkan-sen

Tenkan-sen (the 9-day MA), has managed to cling quite closely to the highs and lows of the daily candles, limiting the very short-term trend fairly nicely. It has held the downside of the last two days, but, should we get a close below here, it would be the first of a series of warning signals that prices might turn lower. At the moment there is nothing in the candles to suggest this is the case.

Moving average crossovers have also worked well, with a hiccup in late August/ early September, and a rather bigger problem from mid-October to early November. At the moment they are unlikely to cross for some time, so the 26-day average is more likely to act as the next support than any reversal sign. Note that when the market traded sideways, this line was not useful at all, with prices spending half their time above it and half below. The likelihood of it providing lasting and clear support looking forward is probably limited.

Clouds performing well

The Clouds have performed well, with prices trading clearly above them in a steadily rising market and limiting downside slides nearly all of the time. The 7 July sudden drop reversed ahead of the top of the Cloud and formed, not quite a hammer, but a fairly powerful reversal candle nevertheless.

Again Senkou Span A stopped pullbacks on 29 August, 22 September (tiny little Doji-type candles just below the top of the Cloud), but fared a lot worse late October.

The low point was again marked by a reversal candle, this time a decent, if not particularly big, hammer. Note also that at this point the Cloud had suddenly become dramatically thinner, a fact that allowed prices to drop below it, but then saw them trade up strongly through it once again.

The Senkou Span lines crossed over in early December: not important, other than the fact the Cloud was extremely thin, and as the market was such a long way from there it is immaterial.

Now the Cloud is getting fatter again and, although we are a very long way from its current level, by mid-January it should have caught up a little with prices and should provide support then.

Chikou Span

Chikou Span, the darker green line, has been more difficult and not so helpful. At the moment it is way above the candle of the 10 November (remember, it is today's closing price plotted 26 days behind). Therefore, candles are unlikely to provide short-term support should the market suddenly dive. On the other hand, there are no candles above it now meaning that resistance is currently non-existent. It can be difficult to use this line retrospectively as one must compare it to where the candles lie 26 days later.

Summary

To summarise, the market is trending higher after a bout of sideways consolidation and there is nothing to suggest a reversal in trend.

Example 2: Euro vs dollar

Now lets look at an example where the market is possibly set to reverse – the euro against the US dollar.

Figure 3-9: Euro against the US dollar

Chart comment

Pushing up into the Cloud for the first time since September.

Analysis

With the exception of a rather dramatic three days in early September, the Cloud has limited rallies most of the time. The Cloud itself was relatively flat in November because the highest price of the last 52 days was the early September high.

Note also that the Cloud has been relatively fat throughout, but has narrowed starting 10 January. Kijun-sen (26-day MA) has flattened suddenly, having dropped very steadily for a long time.

The moving averages themselves have crossed, caused by the strong rally of the 10 December, and are now approaching the bottom of the Cloud which should act as resistance.

Added to the last two days of consecutive candles with long upper shadows in the middle of the Cloud, this hints that we are unlikely to break higher short term, but we will watch in February for a potential uptrend to develop.

In the process Chikou-Span burst higher through the long black candle of the 4 November. It has also broken above both moving averages of 26 days ago and, rather than resistance, these may start providing support. The candles of 26 days ago are some way below Chikou-Span, so if the euro were to slip it could fall quite a long way, but in seven days time these should begin to act as support levels.

Summary

The analysis suggests that the Cloud will therefore limit the upside for another week at least and maybe longer, but there are many elements here suggesting that the longer term picture is setting up for a reversal. I would be watching for more signs that confirm this over the coming month.

This concludes the first and most basic part of this book. Most traders stop here and are happy to limit their analysis to the Clouds and major lines. This is also the case in Japan and is what your average Japanese trader will be watching. In fact, I do too. Then I move back to my more conventional Western methods, which I describe in the next chapter for those of you who are interested.

4

The Three Principles

THE NEXT STEP in Ichimoku Cloud analysis.

The thorough Cloud analyst looks at patterns, waves and calculates price and time targets. These three pillars of the analysis are known as the:

1. Wave Principle
2. Price target
3. Timespan Principle

They must be used simultaneously as they are fundamentally interconnected. For Western analysts much of this will be, if not familiar, then common sense.

Consolidation patterns are likely to take one of several conventional forms. Outlined below are the standard paths that Sanjin Ichimoku felt the market was most likely to follow.

Wave Principle

First, let's look at the consolidation patterns of the Wave Principle.

Although there are many variations of these, they all have the same basic precepts:

- price ranges and wave counts, with wave sizes in proportion to each other;
- breakout price projections based on the sizes of the waves and the consolidation patterns.

In other words, consolidation patterns can be sub-divided into a series of small waves and the size of the pattern determines the extent of the wave that follows on a break-out of the formation.

Figure 4-1: Consolidation patterns of the Wave Principle

One Wave (I)

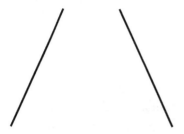

Starting with the simplest wave called an 'I': a market that will either go up in a straight line or down equally steadily, often one wave following the other.

Two Wave (V)

Putting these two together one ends up with pattern 'V', the second simplest one, which may start with an up move which then reverses, or vice versa.

Three Wave (N)

Things get a little more interesting with 'N', which is a three-wave alternating combination either moving up first or down first.

Five Wave (Y, P)

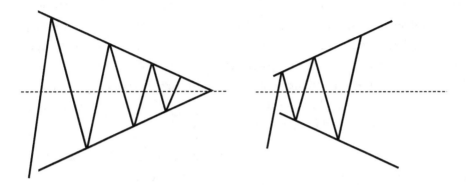

Then we have five wave combinations:

1. The 'P' wave is what we would probably call a triangle, or pennant, formation, where five alternating waves of progressively smaller size can be mapped. These occur in bull and bear markets, with an initial rally in a longer term bull market and kicking off from a low point in a bear market.

2. The 'Y' wave, an alternating five-wave pattern, is what we would probably describe as a broadening top or bottom formation. A triangle-type consolidation whose price swings get larger with time rather than smaller. Again this may start with a rally or with a decline.

Western letters

It is interesting to note the use of Western letters when labelling both the pattern formation and the waves within each. It has been suggested that this was to make the system look more technical and chic. Just as in some emerging market countries where T-shirts have (often misspelt) English slogans emblazoned across them, so too in Japan the use of Western words is seen as trendy. The truth is probably that Chinese characters may not mimic the shape of the moves themselves; for example the N wave (which is up, down, up). Also, Chinese characters do not follow in a series like the Western alphabet (moving from A to Z) and are therefore unsuitable for sequential wave counts. More on this later.

Perhaps rather optimistically, Hosoda believed that every single price move can be resolved into a combination of just these five patterns. In Western technical analysis we use the P and Y patterns as standard, although they occur rarely relative to the whole host of other moves that may be observed, most of which can not be labelled and are seen as general noise. These two patterns are seen as stand alone ones, whereas the other three (I, V, and N) can be used in combinations with each other, succeeding each other.

As well as the basic formations (I, V, and N) Sasaki added one of his own called a '4', as it is a four-step formation, again where the first leg can start with either a rally or a decline. So, P and Y are used on their own. The other four wave types, which have two variations each (up first or down first), can be combined together to form composite wave formations.

The diagrams below give you some idea as to how quickly these can mutate into many different forms. So the basic building blocks are able to create an infinite number of potential market paths. Now you can see what is beginning to look like the type of moves we so often see in the charts.

Figure 4-2: Wave variations

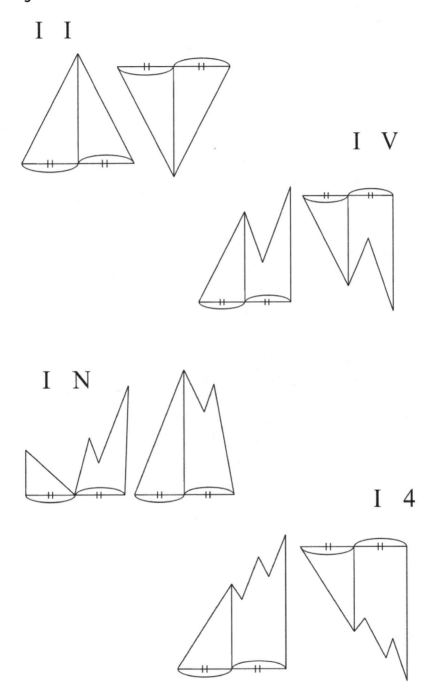

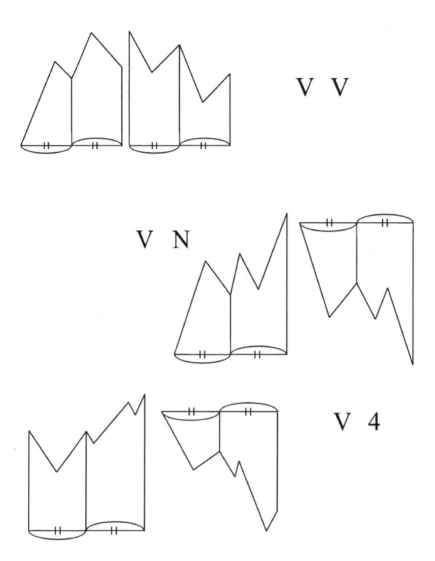

N N

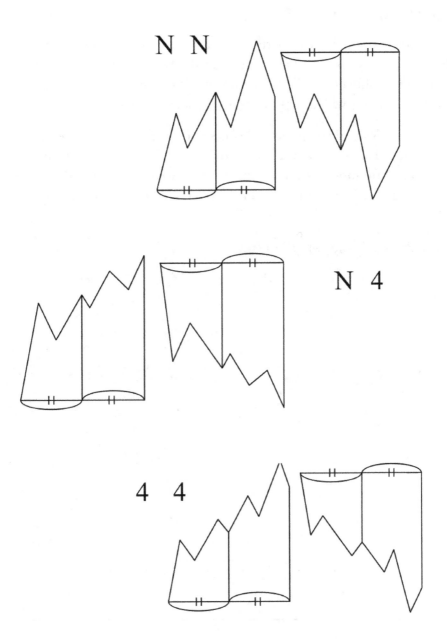

N 4

4 4

No limit to the number of waves

Long-term trends, which are constructed with these basic building blocks, are labelled sequentially, using either numbers or the Western alphabet. There is no limit to the number of waves needed to complete a long-term move, unlike the short-term moves which must be in single, double or triple waves.

Unlike in Elliott Wave theory, where all rallies must work out as five alternating waves higher, and all bear markets three moves lower, Hosoda was quite happy to count long-term moves as threes, fives or even twenty waves (labelled with letters A through to Z potentially or an infinite number of sequential digits!)

Figure 4-3: Thai baht per US dollar

Chart comment

Sequential labelling of the waves that make up a trend.

Figure 4-4: Korean won per US dollar

Chart comment

Alphabetic labelling of the waves where the trend is not so clear.

Personally, I do not feel these are true wave counts, as Westerners understand them. I think Sasaki is merely marking intermediate highs and lows in some way so that these can be pinpointed clearly, prior to further analysis and classification into the different pattern types.

Weekly rather than daily candles

I believe that the wave counts work much better with weekly, rather than daily, candles. Certainly important highs and strong reversal patterns are often clearer to spot on weekly charts. From these wave counts are easier to agree on and the analysis has a better chance of success. I always give more weight to candle formations on monthly and weekly charts rather than daily ones.

As you can see, Japanese technical analysts bend the rules – so feel free to experiment!

Figure 4-5: Weekly S&P 500

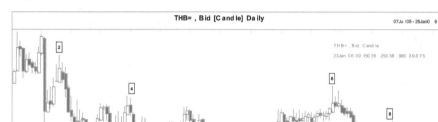

Chart comment

Numbering the waves in a bull market.

The list below is merely how many weeks it took to get from one numbered point to the next. So from point 1 on the chart it took four weeks to get to point 2. From 2 to 3, ten or 11 weeks, depending on which of the two equal highs you choose. Wave 7' is explained below. The reason for calculating the intervals between points will become clear when we discuss the Timespan Principle.

1-2=4	2-6=28/29
2-3=10/11	6-8=26/27
3-4=4	3-7=33
4-5=7	7-9=25
5-6=7	1-3=14/15
6-7=15/16	3-6=18
7-8=11	6-8=26/27
7'-8=6	5-7=22/23
8-9=14	5-7'=27

Wave counts were then adapted to include highs and lows at the same level while keeping the structure of the patterns. In this case successive highs or lows at the same level are marked with an apostrophe. So wave A precedes wave A', or wave 1 precedes wave 1'. We could liken this to Elliott Wave theory where an X is used to label an extra wave or extension.

Figure 4-6: Hungarian forints per euro

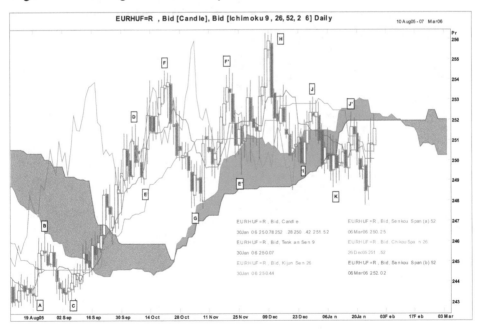

Chart comment

Alphabetically labelled wave count in a currency pair that is moving broadly sideways. Note the E', F', and J'.

Resistance becomes support

As in Dow Theory, what had been resistance becomes support, and vice versa. The top of a rally then provides support for pullbacks following a break to new highs. Therefore waves are more likely to turn at support and resistance levels. This point is labelled 'S' – presumably for support.

Figure 4-7: Resistance becomes support

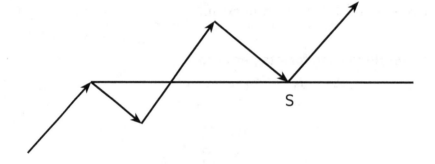

Figure 4-8: Example of crude oil demonstrating resistance becoming support

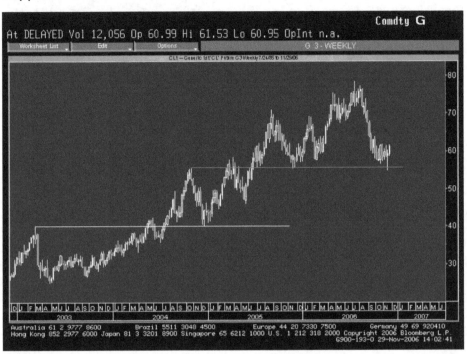

Conclusion

The Wave Principle has two parts to it:

1. Of lesser importance is the labelling of intermediate highs and lows, either with letters or with numbers. As there is no limit to the number of moves, the process seems a bit irrelevant. The only use I can see for this is to make it easier to then subdivide the long-term trend into the component short-term wave structures.

2. More controversially all and every consolidation pattern can be subdivided into a combination of structures labelled I, V, N, P, and Y, plus Mr. Sasaki's '4'.

Price targets

From the N Wave consolidation patterns, price targets are determined. Again, this should be straightforward, as it uses measurements of the size of the whole pattern and the size of each of the waves within it. As in Western technical analysis, the height of the triangle gives a target price for when we break out of the pattern. Similarly a head-and-shoulders pattern gives a price target and Elliott Wave theory states that wave C will be in proportion to wave A lower.

Ichimoku targets can only cope with the size of the very next little wave. Each consolidation pattern suggests the direction of the very next move only. It does not predict the next series of waves and long-term targets as Elliott Wave can do. So, one step at a time here.

The price targets are labelled V, N, E, and NT. The first two are self-evident – being the final leg of their respective formations. E may have stemmed from the fact the pattern has two equal halves, where the last leg compensates for the dip to C, but this is unclear. I can only imagine Hosoda-san ran out of ideas when labelling the last one NT.

Figure 4-9: Price targets

1

$V = B + (B - C)$

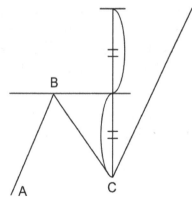

2

$N = C + (B - A)$

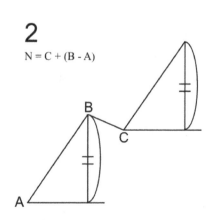

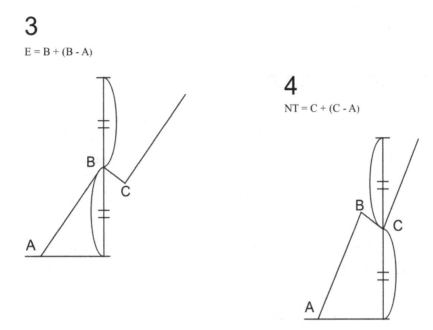

3

$E = B + (B - A)$

4

$NT = C + (C - A)$

Limited use of price targets

To be frank, I hardly ever use the price target part of the analysis at all. I find it far too fiddly and overly simplistic. Something of a straightjacket. I also dislike the fact that it predicts such a relatively short price and time ahead. This is all very well for very active rice traders perhaps, and when you are only looking at a very few financial instruments. But for investors, and those who want to take a longer term view, it has little value. Also it makes it very difficult to decide whether a trade is worth doing – the 'reward' side of a risk/reward measure is likely to be small because such a short time frame is used. However, this is perhaps worth investigating further using weekly candles.

In terms of price targets I tend to stick to traditional Western methods. I do however think that for very active traders who only cover a very limited number of instruments this Japanese version is superior. One can be far more precise and capture a lot more of the intra-day price moves and trade profitably in periods of congestion.

Of far more interest are the cyclical underpinnings of the Timespan Principle, which we come to next.

Timespan Principle

Key to this is the idea of special numbers. Not lucky ones as 7, or unlucky 13, but ones which, from number crunching, are considered significant. We are not going into the realms of mysticism here, as those of you who are aficionados of Fibonacci retracements and projections will understand. Proportions of 0.61875 and 0.38125 are also special, but not magical (although some do believe 1.618 is divine).

The Timespan Principle has three simple numbers: 9, 17 and 26 (remember, 9 and 26 are the days used for the moving averages) and are considered the most useful:

- **9** is known as the 'basic unit'
- **17** (9+9-1) is two of these basis units (the −1 is explained later)
- **26** is three basic units (9+9+9-1), or one 'term unit'.

The next set of numbers are compound ones, arrived at through rough combinations of the first three. These are:

- 33 (one term unit plus one basic unit), 26+9-1
- 42 (one term unit plus seventeen), 26+17-1
- 65 (is known as one 'super big unit'), 33+33-1
- 76, (known as one 'cycle' as well as being three 'term units'), 26+26+26-2
- 129, 65+65-1
- 172, 65+42+42+26-3
- 257, 129+129-1

You can see that the word 'roughly' is very appropriate.

Avoiding double-counting

One digit is deducted because: "it has one attachment part". This is in order to avoid double counting the candle that lies on the last day of the first section and is the first day of the second part of the sum. So for compound number

172=(65+42+42+26-3), we deduct three days' worth of candles, one for each day between the four counting periods.

At first these compound numbers may seen a bit confusing, but the following may help.

Let's say we start with a series of nine ascending candles which we have labelled 1 to 9. Then one observes a series of descending candles labelled A to I. You will note that candle 9 and A are one and the same. The whole of this inverted V wave pattern is completed at the seventeenth candle.

Figure 4-10: Inverted V wave pattern

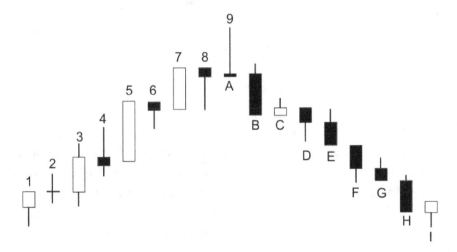

Now let's look at an N wave which starts with nine ascending candles forming the first leg. The down move also consists of nine candles, as does the last leg higher. These have again been numbered for rallies and labelled with letters on the way down. As before, the first candle 9 and A are one and the same, and similarly I and the second 1 are also the same Hammer candle. The whole formation takes 25 days to complete and in order not to double count the candles at the turning points the formula is: (9+9+9-2)=25.

Figure 4-11: N wave pattern

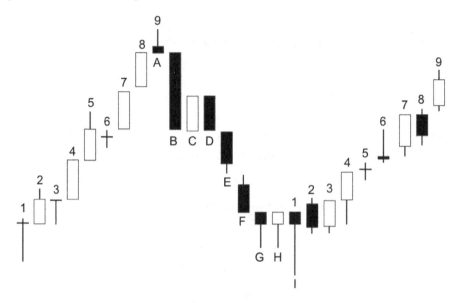

Projecting ahead

Just as economic cycles are said to range from 3.5 years all the way through to 54 years, highs and lows on the path to prosperity lie at regular intervals along the way. Similarly Fibonacci numbers can be used to predict certain dates in the future. Say the latest move from a high at A to a low at B took 10 days, then Fibonacci time projections would mark 6 (0.6 x 10), 10 (1 x 10), and 16 (1.6 x 10) days ahead as being days where the trend may change again.

Ichimoku day counts are plotted from intermediate highs and lows and we watch for where they cluster in the future. The more counts that end at, or close to, the same day in the future, the more likely that that day will see a trend end and reverse. Again, all these numbers were discovered through trial and error - in what must have been a nightmare job.

Kihon Suchi

Timespan numbers are used to project how many days ahead an interim high or low is likely to occur, known as Kihon Suchi, or "the day of the turn". So, from an important low of what should be an N pattern, if A to B took 9 days then point C will be 17 days ahead (9+9-1) of point A, and point D, 25 days from the start date (9+9+9-2). The N formation should then finish when the third wave matches the height of the first one and around 9 days after point C.

From the completed N wave the next move might be an I wave lower which should take about 26 days (one of the preferred day counts). This is so that the I formation most closely mirrors the size of the N wave which took 26 days to develop.

Figure 4-12: Kihon Suchi

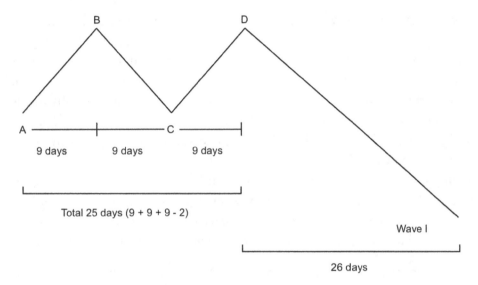

When working out day counts these do not necessarily have to succeed each other perfectly. Hosoda-san allowed for gaps in the count: say, one to five days, around important highs or lows. As already mentioned markets are more likely to reverse/accelerate around the time when the Clouds become very thin, so too the day counts start from around the time of significant highs and lows. Of course, this makes it a lot easier to fit the 9, 17, 33 day counts to what has actually happened. It also makes it far harder to decide exactly on a date in the future when the move will end.

Not to be treated with too much precision

Note again the qualifying use of the word 'about'. All of these are indications and are not cast in concrete; one must allow for a day or two either side of each and every number, coupled with the fact you are subtracting for the attachment parts. Just as the Clouds give you some idea when the trend may change, so too do these projections. For example, after an important high one might expect 33 or 42 days while the market pulls back and consolidates.

Intuitively, the 9 day and 26 day numbers make sense, 9 being just under two weeks and 26 what had been the average working month. These are similar to 10 and 20-day moving averages used by many Westerners.

Timing is implicit in the pattern analysis

Beyond that, I feel there are simply too many potential turning dates to cope with. Cyclical analysts will beg to differ, but I feel that a more flexible view suits me. For example, if a dramatic Shooting Star reversal candle forms, I would rather go with that and forget about all possible day counts. And what if the move turns out to have an extension? Where do I then start my subsequent day count? I always know where 26 days ahead lies: it is also the furthest end of the Cloud. Thirty-three days ahead is just a few more, so again you might start guessing what the Cloud might look like on that day. If, say, it has been getting thinner over the last week or so, then I assume it will become more so by then. So here, while I am looking at where important turning points might lie, it is the Cloud itself rather than the wave counts or price targets that are the basis of my view; if and when the two coincide the likelihood increases.

Western pattern analysis also gives hints at dates ahead when things are about to change. For example, a head-and-shoulders top: the perfect (idealised) example of which will be symmetrical and have a horizontal neckline. If the left shoulder took three weeks to form, and the top of the head was two weeks after the first neckline point, then the rest of the formation will probably take five weeks to complete – two weeks to the second neckline point and three weeks to form the right shoulder. Again, in a perfect world it will be the same height as the first one. In other words, as in Ichimoku charts, the timing aspect is also inherent in some conventional pattern analysis.

Figure 4-13: Head and shoulders pattern

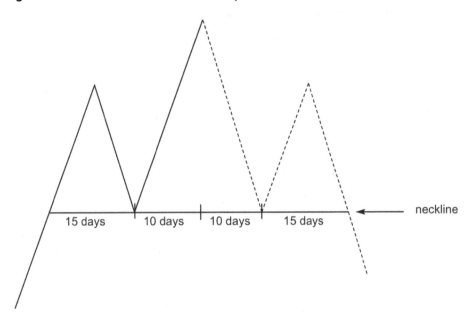

9, 17 and 26 – the most useful day counts

I think most Japanese traders would agree that the dates that are most useful for the timing part of this analysis are the 9, 17 and 26. Often 44 days seems to work quite well, but in my opinion not often enough to make it truly crucial.

Figure 4-14: CAC40 index with Time Principle days ahead plotted from an interim low on the 28 October

Chart comment

Plotting the number of days ahead gives us some idea as to where intermediate as well as major market turns might occur. It is a rather laborious process though.

A great deal of subjectivity is involved

I know that some Japanese traders feel there is too much subjectivity involved in combining the day counts and the wave counts. One dealer may feel that the formation starts on the exact day of the time analysis, while another would prefer to start with the last significant high or low. Depending on the initial choice, and add in the fact that one can use some leeway with the day count, the two dealers would end up with different price and time targets. A similar question arises with the numbering or lettering of the waves. Where interim highs and lows are close, but not exactly the same, should these be labelled

A' or B, 2', or 3? My gut feeling is that this might lead to the kind of lengthy discussions most often heard in Elliott Wave circles.

Also remember that over time markets and instruments change and some methods of analysis will work better under certain conditions. Do not be afraid to discard methods when you feel the market has changed. For example:

- For very explosive markets which are trending very strongly, I immediately discard the Relative Strength Index.

- When markets are in very strong bull or bear moves, I tend to discard all wave counts, and therefore most price targets. Nevertheless, I keep an eye on time targets.

Likewise in sideways moves I will discard moving averages and the Ichimoku Cloud.

Figure 4-15: Front month sugar futures contract New York Board of Trade

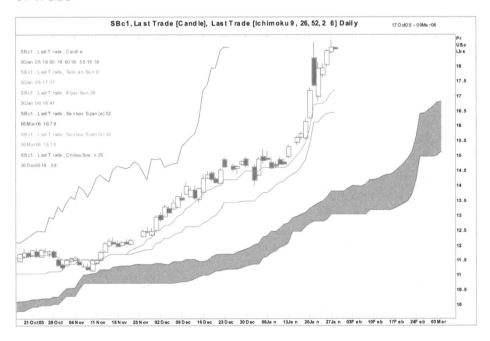

Chart comment

Explosive move higher and very dynamic despite a thin Cloud.

The chart of sugar above is a good example of a massive move where rigid analysis ought to be discarded, be it Ichimoku Kinko, RSI or pattern analysis.

That's the end of looking at the three principles of Cloud analysis. We'll next turn to applying all this in practice and work through some real-life case studies.

5

Case Studies

Now THE DIFFICULT part of putting all this into practice. In the following pages we will work through in detail how we would use all the Ichimoku Kinko Hyo tools, remembering the vital link between time and price.

Just to remind you (in case you have got lost by now), the elements we have to consider are:

1. the candles themselves,

2. 9 and 26-day moving averages,

3. the Cloud and its size,

4. Chikou Span,

5. the long-term wave count,

6. the short-term wave count,

7. the Wave Principle,

8. Price targets, and

9. Time Principle.

Phew, and you thought this was the easy answer to your prayers!

Study 1: FTSE 100 Index

I have deliberately chosen a complex example so that you are not lulled into a false sense of security. Too many textbooks use charts that work perfectly, and the reader becomes frustrated or angry when reality turns out to be different from the theoretical examples. I think it is better to understand the complexity of the work first and then decide if you can face continuing with it. Remember, markets are not easy and making money even harder.

Figure 5-1: FTSE 100 index

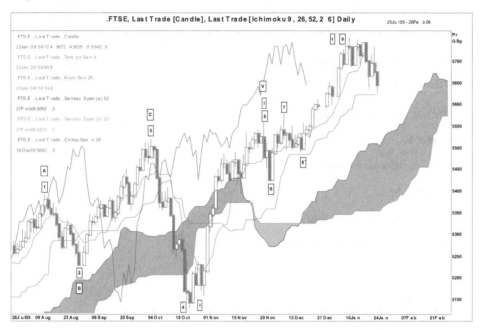

Before making predictions we have to go back over the chart and see what has been happening, labelling moves as appropriate. Mark the important interim highs and lows (in the chart above labelled 1-9). Note that in this example you cannot see what happened before August, so it would probably be a good idea to look further back for more price history before doing the labelling.

Identify the wave patterns

Moves **1**, **2** and **3** form the A, B and C legs of an N pattern. The top at 3 is equal in size to wave 1 measured from the point where it breaks above the high at 1 (an E-type price target). Go back and make sure you have understood this bit.

Wave 4 is an I wave which dips into the middle of the Cloud, bounces a little to stall at the top of the Cloud, then hurtles lower to break below the bottom of the Cloud.

The move ends with a very unusual reversal-type candle (Doji), the day before the low point at 4. Note that on this day Chikou Span almost holds against the bottom of the Cloud of that day (18 September and 26 days before point 4).

76

Wave 5 higher starts dramatically, because it is so far below the Cloud, and then moves more slowly clinging to the top of the Cloud in early November. It is another I pattern whose size and timing (26 days up following wave 4's 15 days down) are related.

Waves 4 and 5 combine into a V pattern and follow the N combination.

Rather more subjective is **wave 6** which is a lot smaller than all the previous ones, and perhaps we ought to have labelled 7 as a 5'. With the labelling as per the chart above, **waves 6, 7, and 8** form another N pattern, this time one that starts with a down move and where the second downside price objective at 8 falls short of its target. Perhaps this little cluster should be seen as an attempt to establish support roughly in the area which had been resistance at 3 and the top of wave C, and point 6 becomes the S for support. Subjectivity has already crept in. Note how the moving averages contain price action in this little section and then move on up steadily, supporting the rally neatly on the next move higher to 9.

Wave 9 is another I that takes 15 days to complete with a little Doji candle at the very top.

The latest move lower has so far been contained by the moving averages, not the 9 day, but the 26 day one. Because the latest move was an I following an N, there is a good chance that the next move will be an I lower of about 17 days, which is 31 January 2006. Observe where the top of the Cloud lies on that day as it might stem the flow. The other possibility is that wave 9 is the first leg of another N wave and then we would end up with an N, N combination of waves.

Projections

Projecting out into the future, we shall use the high at 3, low at 4, and high at 9 as our most important dates.

To point 3 (3 October) and point 4 (21 October) we shall add 42, 65, 76 and 129 days. To point 9 (9 January) we add 9, 17, 26, 33 and 42 days. Working these all out laboriously with a calendar we look to see where dates may cluster. According to my calculations, dates to watch will be the 18 and 29 January and 13 February. On 23 January 2006 the high at 9 is holding and could mean that we are forming an interim top between the 18 and 29 January.

Note that Chikou Span is currently well above the Cloud and candles, and has no overhead resistance – so no impediments to upward progress here. Prices are currently well above the Cloud and the Senkou Spans have flattened out recently; a little worrying as, if prices continue to move sideways, the Cloud could become very thin quite quickly. These indicators do not signal a potential reversal in the upward trend yet. However, should there be a sudden drop, as we saw in early October, it could be very large indeed as the top of the Cloud lies at 5500 and the bottom of it at 5350.

Conclusion

The trend higher should continue, because the Clouds, Chikou Span and moving averages (despite these flattening out) are pointing higher. The wave and date counts hint that we may suffer a sudden slide towards 5500 somewhere between late January and mid-February.

I am beginning to struggle with the wave counts, feeling very uncertain about my labelling of 5,6,7 and 8. Perhaps I ought to have counted the move from 4 to 9 as one bigger move. If this were the case, then any decline is likely to last for longer and be much bigger in size than currently estimated. I am also worried that point 9 may turn out not to be an intermediate high at all, and that it is merely a stalling point in a longer term uptrend.

Study 2: Short sterling interest rate future

For those of you who are not familiar with money market interest rate futures contracts, the price of these is 100 minus three-month LIBOR (London Inter Bank Offered Rate). These contracts were devised so that pit traders could make money by buying the futures when yields went down, and selling them when yields went up.

For example, if rates are currently 5.00%, the futures contract would be priced as 100.00-5.00 = 95.00. If rates were then to drop to 4.00%, the contract would be priced at 100.00-4.00 = 96.00. The trader would have made 100 basis points (1.00%) by buying at 95.00 and selling at 96.00. Just like many novice FX traders, some people find it difficult to buy, say, Swiss francs at CHF 1.2600 to the US dollar, and make money by selling them out again at 1.2500. Now you can see why almost every time bonds are mentioned in newspapers, the words "as prices go up yields go down" are usually added.

In the short sterling example (chart below) I have chosen to use weekly candles to see if this makes the wave count any easier. So that readers understand what happened before this picture was snapped, the market had traded up from a low at 94.00 in June 2002, to a high at 96.00 in June 2003, then back down to 94.20 in June 2004. In other words, expectations for where interest rates would be in March 2006 have fluctuated wildly between 6.00% and 4.00%.

Figure 5-2: Short sterling interest rate future (Euronext.liffe)

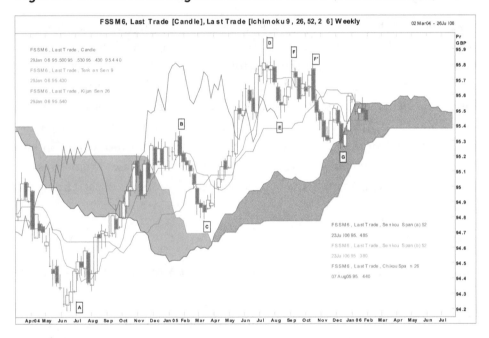

Analysis

In this slow, upwardly trending market, moving averages worked pretty well while prices were rallying, the nine-week one hugging price action until July 2005. But as the market appears to be moving broadly sideways at the moment we shall ignore the moving averages for now.

The Clouds have been fairly decisive and fat all along, except at the point where the Spans cross. Note that it is at this point that prices were at their closest to the Cloud, having held well above it since December 2004. The top of the Cloud limited the downside in December 2005, but is not doing quite such a good job at the moment. The Cloud moves across the page from February 2006 until July, almost horizontally and in a tight, clearly defined band. The reason the Clouds are flat for so long is that unless a new low is posted, the last significant low to be used for calculations is the one of the last 52 weeks.

The chances of a market keeping neatly between 95.40 and 95.60 for the next seven months are slim. The Cloud also gets even thinner mid-July, suggesting prices are more likely to break through it then.

Prediction

Over the next few weeks the market will probably remain trapped inside the Cloud itself, with dips to the lower edge seen as a medium-term buying opportunity as the long term trend is still up. Chikou Span is rather a mess at the moment: trading in the middle of the broad price band established since July 2005. Plenty of resistance, starting at 95.60 which is just above the top of the Cloud today, so there is perhaps a short-term trading opportunity here. The relatively tight range might continue for another three months as Chikou Span weaves its way slowly through the candles. The candles themselves are not interesting at the moment, but do note the Shooting Star at D and the Doji at E.

Wave patterns

Now let's look at the patterns. The move down to A marks the end of a long-term decline.

The rally **from A to D** is an N - an upward sloping one and a very dynamic move where the second leg travels the same price distance as the first. A to B takes 33 weeks, C to D, 18. Note that B to C is 8 weeks, making the composite number of 57=(33+18+8-2) for the whole of the N pattern.

Waves E, F, and G build another downward N, this time a slightly more complex one as there is a wave F', some sort of shadow of F, which confuses the time count too. Counting the weeks lower from F', the move took 9 weeks, while wave E took 6, and they both covered exactly the same distance in price. The low point at G comes 23 weeks after D, 41 weeks after C, and 81 weeks after A. Perhaps the low at G is significant as it is very close to the high at B.

In this case, it might be the S point where what had been resistance, becomes support. The Cloud also helps here.

Summary

From all of the above I would conclude that prices are likely to crawl sideways within the Cloud for the next few weeks at least. My bias would be for a subsequent slow move higher as G is likely to be an important interim low. Upside pressure would increase if prices went on to hold above the Cloud and/or if Chikou Span managed to climb back clearly above the candles. I would probably favour an upward sloping N move staring at G over the next 17 to 26 weeks taking the market back up towards D, the 7 July high.

Study 3: CADUSD

The next should hopefully be an easier example: the Canadian dollar against the US dollar quoted as Canadian dollars per greenback. Here we are using a daily candlestick chart. Note that since January 2002's all-time high at C$1.6180 the exchange rate has moved steadily lower: increasing the value of the 'loonie' (as the Canadian dollar is known) by 40% against its US counterpart. Also note that C$1.1200 was the strongest the Canadian dollar got to against the US$ (1991) in the last 25 years. So at 1.1500 we are perilously close to historical key support, after a precipitous decline in the value of the US dollar.

Having marked in our intermediate highs and lows with letters this time (numbers and letters are really interchangeable), note that there are many waves marked with an asterisk. This shows how well recent highs are working in terms of creating neat resistance levels.

Figure 5-3: Canadian dollars per US dollar

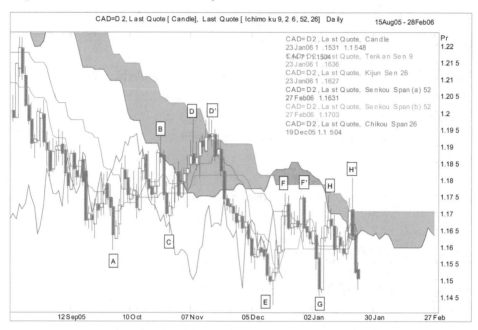

Analysis

Moving averages were in a steady downtrend until October and the Clouds continued pushing lower until mid-December. Both of these are currently mixed at best, although the Cloud has dipped again. Nevertheless, even when the Cloud was very thin, its upper edge has done an excellent job at limiting most upside probes, often creating dramatic reversal candle formations (a Doji at B, Shooting Stars at D, D', H and a combination of Shooting Star with Bearish engulfing at H'). This last candle is particularly strong and being the fourth in a series of tops at the same level must be treated with a lot of respect. The Cloud is becoming thicker and has a clearly defined horizontal top at 1.1700. Perhaps the Cloud will start to turn lower again soon as the high at D' drops out after 52 days, and the bottom edge will slip faster than the top one if we move to a new low price.

Chikou Span has edged well below the candles of 26 days ago and has a lot of overhead resistance to contend with all the way up to 1.1800. This suggests that, despite the potential for more consolidation between 1.1450 and 1.1700, eventually the next move will be lower.

The patterns are very difficult to see because there are so many shadow wave counts. The move from D to E is an **I wave** that took 22 days to complete. The subsequent move from E to H is probably best labelled as an upward sloping **N**, where E to F is the same price size as G to H, and has almost the same day count (an I, N combination). Now I would favour another **I wave** lower starting at H'.

Prediction

Because we are so close to historical long-term lows the next move might be an N. The dynamic of a potential **I wave** is curtailed by an historic low at 1.1200, so we may well get a more lengthy consolidation above here for the move to resume later on. Nerves are likely to be rattled if this pair moves to parity, something I see as a real possibility long term.

Study 4: Gold

The price of gold, in US dollars for spot delivery, will be the basis of our next detailed example. We will be using the daily chart, but because it has moved so much over the last two years I have also included a weekly one for the historical context.

Readers should be aware that after languishing in the doldrums for much of the late 1990s and early this century, suspension of central bank sales coupled with massive speculative interest has seen prices soar, particularly over the last twelve months. Price action for this period, our daily chart, is especially violent and nothing like what it usually is: soaring to a high at $730 in early May, followed by an especially sharp drop over the next 24 days.

So let's see how Ichimoku charts cope with extreme conditions.

Figure 5-4: Gold (weekly), for historical reference

Figure 5-5: Gold (daily)

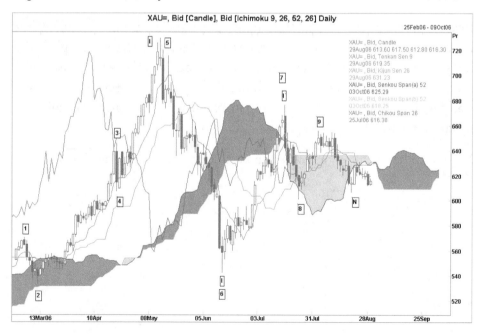

Analysis

First things first: let's label the important intermediate highs and lows. Here they are one to nine. April's explosive rally is obviously an **I wave**, as is the subsequent collapse. Forty-six days up from the mid-March low (where the lower edge of the Cloud provided neat support) culminating in a Doji candle and a large dark one on the day after that. Quite a powerful little duo, I would say.

Three days after the top at 5 we get a Shooting Star, adding considerable downside momentum.

The top of the Cloud slows things down a little in early June, but prices then plummet dramatically – ridiculously so! A low of $543, so a loss of $187 or 25% over 24 working days. It just goes to show what happens when too much hot money without deep pockets gets obsessed with the same thing.

This second **I wave** took us all the way back down to where we started off in March but twice as quickly as the previous rally (24 versus 46 days). These two waves put together form a **V wave**.

The drop culminates in a Hammer candle and on this day Chikou Span hits the Cloud of 26 days earlier which provides support all the way up for the next 24 days (again 24 days).

I have labelled this third wave as another **I** but I'm not nearly as sure about this as I was with the last two. It certainly tops dramatically, with a Bearish engulfing candle just above the top of the Cloud, because at this point Spans A and B cross. How else might I label the waves from point 6 onwards?

From the Hammer at 6 up to 7, then down 8 and back up to 9 might all form an **N wave** (which did not meet its price objective).

Then we are left with the most recent decline which I'm not sure how to label at all. Or might the N wave start at 7, down to 8, up to 9 and down again? Size and shape-wise this looks better. Then the rally from $543 to $676 is another I. Whatever we decide I think the most salient feature of the period between mid-June and now is that it is a **consolidation phase** with a series of corrective waves that form a triangle. Price action is very different from that of March to June when clear trends were in place. This market is looking for direction.

My gut instinct is to almost ignore all the little moves from point 7 onwards because these are irrelevant noise.

Referring to Elliott Waves, I would suggest that everything after point 5 is corrective and that we are forming a large A, B, C-type Elliott wave count. If 9 is merely a shadow of 7, then the next move should be lower to form Elliott's C wave. This could then be counted as the last part of a very large **N wave** that started at 5 (leg one down to 6 and two up to 7).

Predictions

Based on this alternative count, what are my price and time targets?

The first leg of this N that starts downwards took 24 days, as did the subsequent rally to 7. From 7 to 9 takes 12 days, and if this move is an extension then 36 days in total for the second leg of the big N. If the next wave lower started at 7 then it is likely to take 42 days; if it starts at 9 then it is more likely to take 26 days or so. Measuring these out my target dates would be between the 6th and the 12th of September. Note that the Cloud gets a lot thicker by then, and despite being very thin at the moment prices are currently holding neatly below the Cloud.

My price target for this decline will probably be the $540/$560 area again.

How did I get to this magic number?

If this next move were the same size as the first one ($187), then prices would tumble to $500. This is probably overkill and quite a feat in less than three weeks. If this N wave has legs of different sizes, like the first case study, then the third leg should travel the distance between points B and C of the drawing. In other words, on the gold chart I measure the distance between the Hammer of early June to the Bearish engulfing candle of mid-July ($543 to $676 equals $133). Dropping $133 from point 7 gets me back down to $543, where we reversed sharply with the large Hammer. In other words, a slightly truncated third leg which would, in Elliott-speak, make the C wave 0.618% of the A wave.

At what point would I decide that my outlook was wrong?

Moving averages are currently of no use, but the Cloud is. If prices were to hold persistently above Senkou Span A, and so too was Chikou Span (not just the odd blip), then I would certainly start sweating.

And what if we were to drop below $540, what then?

I would watch for another very dramatic reversal candle(s). I also know that the weekly Cloud lies at $510 with its lower edge at $475, rising quickly to $625 by year-end. Once I have a base established I would see this as an excellent opportunity to re-buy for another long-term move back over the $700 mark.

Study 5: USDYEN

The next example is very different: daily dollar/yen quoted in the European orientation, as how many yen you need to buy one US dollar.

Price action has been very contained over the period – March 2006 to date with a mean of 115.00, one standard deviation around here being 2 yen or 1.75% either side of the mean. Once again I have labelled the important(ish) highs and lows sequentially from one to twelve, noting that there are quite a few apostrophe counts. The moves up to 1, down to 2, and back up to 1' obviously form an N formation that took 9, 6, and 17 days for each leg. Note the Shooting Star' six days before 1' warning you that despite appearances things are getting unsteady. Moving averages and Clouds are not much use as the market is moving sideways.

Figure 5-6: USDYEN (daily)

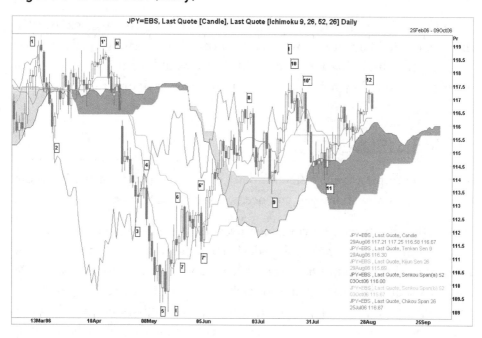

Analysis

But look how the Cloud comes in to its own at the end of April. After clinging just above the top of the Cloud for most of the month, prices suddenly slide to the bottom of it and then gap lower with a very large dark candle when prices break below Senkou Span B. The price plummets (because there is no support) for 18 days after breaking the Cloud, taking a total of 27 days to get from 1' to 5 in an **I wave**. A large Bullish engulfing candle marks the low at 5, its bullish implications balanced to a certain extent with an inverted Hammer at 6. This leads to a period of consolidation above the 9-day moving average and a Doji at 6', but prices hold at 7'.

Apostrophe waves are to be expected in consolidation phases and instruments with relatively small moves.

Then the rally continues on to 8 piercing the Cloud because it has got very thin.

It is interesting to note how the Cloud gets steadily fatter during June, with a horizontal upper edge which limits dips in the price from 14 June to the end of July.

Look at the little Hammer at 9. I have labelled the move from 5 to 10 as another I making 1' to 10 a **V combination**.

August has again seen the Cloud limit the downside and we are now in an **N wave** that starts by moving lower: 10 to 11 the first leg, 11 to 12 the second, and now we are looking for price action to form a top at 12.

Where and when will this occur?

From the Hammer at 9 it takes eight days to get to a small Bearish engulfing/ Spike high candle at 10. From here another five days to 10', plus another nine days to point 11 – a total of 13 days. Since then we have spent 16 days climbing, very laboriously, back up towards the high at 10. The top of the Cloud has limited the daily lows and I am not at all sure that my label at 12 is correct.

So why do it, you ask?

Because we are 17 days after point 11; because price action since the 9 low is consolidation; if 11 to 12 were to be equal to the size of the price move from 9 to 10, then we should top around 118.45. One way or another, I am expecting dollar/yen to top now in terms of price and time.

And after that?

The Cloud is still thick, but narrows dramatically towards the end of September. So maybe we should allow for another month's worth of slow cautious moves – probably another tiny **N** clinging to the top of the Cloud. When, if I am correct, the Cloud is decisively broken expect another I wave because this market has been alternating between big(ish) moves and tiny ones.

How low might we go?

If **I** waves 1' to 5 and 5 to 10 each took the price down and then up by about 9 to 10 yen, let's opt for the same again, giving a target of roughly 108.00, and third time lucky!

For your information, most of the business in this currency pair originates in Tokyo or from Japanese companies. As most of the dealers handling these orders use Ichimoku charts, I would be shooting myself in the foot if I chose to ignore the Clouds when analysing this currency pair.

Study 6: Dow Jones Utilities Index

My next example is the Dow Jones Utilities Index and as it may be one some of you are not familiar with I have also included a weekly chart, although the analysis has been done only with the daily chart. It is a price-weighted index of 15 utility companies listed on the New York Stock Exchange and started at 50 in January 1929.

Note how well the weekly Clouds have worked in this year's consolidation phase. Sticking with the weekly chart you will see that the index saw an explosive rally starting in May 2004 to late 2005, admittedly from very depressed levels (remember, this index used to include the likes of Enron), almost doubling in value over that period. *Who said utility companies were quasi-bonds whose dividends were equivalent to coupons!*

Figure 5-7: Dow Jones Utilities Index (weekly)

Figure 5-8: Dow Jones Utilities Index (daily)

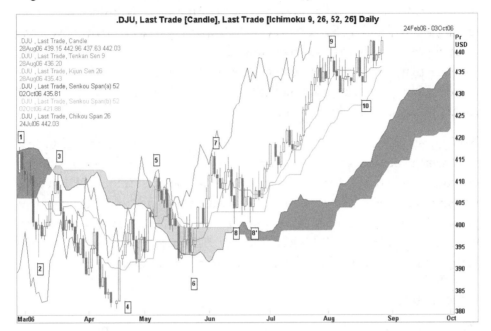

Analysis

Back to work on the daily chart, keeping in mind the above.

Same old formula: label the important intermediate highs and lows. By now I have decided that I prefer numbers rather than letters, as it's easier to make notes of the wave patterns and keep them separate. One to 9', but I realise that some may question my point 10 (and whether 9' is an important interim top).

At 1 the top of the Cloud holds admirably with almost a Bearish engulfing candle on the subsequent day. Five days after point 1 we get a giant black candle that crashes below the bottom of the Cloud. A Hammer or massive Spike low at 2 starts a corrective bounce which is limited very neatly by a rather thin Cloud at 3. Down steadily for the next 22 days to point 4 making this an **N wave** (8+7+22 days −2=35) that takes a total of 35 days to complete; the third leg is just a little bigger in price than the first move lower.

A minute Hammer at 4, coupled with a massive white candle, starts off the next rally which stalls under the Cloud four days later but then manages to get a hair's breadth above the top of it at 5. Then prices have a lot more trouble with the top of the Cloud and cling below Senkou Span B all the way down to the Hammer at 6 (note how the day's closing price is inside the Cloud leaving a long dangling Spike low at 6). Rallying very quickly back above a not especially fat Cloud two days later and holding neatly above it throughout June. I believe that from 4 to 7 is another **N wave** (15+14+7 days −2=34), a 34-day move matching the time taken in the first **N** formation. The distance travelled (price) from 4 to 5 is (almost) equal to 6 to 7.

Now things change and we have a serious, steady long rally from 8 to 9, an **I wave** which takes a decent 35 days (again!). Note that I have deliberately skipped over the mess between 8 and 8', which is possibly the most minute **N**, but adds nothing to the chart. Anyway, the strong rally ending at 9 took the index to a new all-time high, just above the previous peak of December 2000. Considering we are at such lofty levels I think it prudent to label 442.96, the newest all-time high, as a 9' and I shall allow for some hesitation around current prices.

Predictions

We are currently way above a very thick Cloud and the 26-day moving average has done a splendid job for a long time. There is nothing to hinder Chikou Span's way up – on the contrary, August's candles should provide support for this line, and thereby support for price action over the coming month, just as they did from mid-May to early June. I will expect a series of small, slow, cautious moves over the next four weeks where hopefully the top of the Cloud will also provide support because it is so thick.

Then up again to new all-time highs. Really?, you will probably say, knowing that the Dow Jones Industrial Average and S&P 500 are struggling under this year's highs and under all-time highs. Yes, why not? This index of just 15 shares has a special value to investors who have belatedly woken up to its attractions.

The long term wave and Cloud situation suggest a rally to 500/540. How am I sure you ask, as this would represent an almost 25% increase in value.

OK, let's slow down and cover the short- and medium-term prognosis.

Short and medium term

Remember, the Wave Principle only predicts the next few small moves, not a big picture view like this. Starting at 9, we had a first leg lower and a cautious drop to the 430.00 area and a Spike low at point 10. Then rallied over the next four days to 9'. We now will probably break below the nine-day and 26-day moving averages, frightening short-term traders and those scared of heights, but there is plenty of Cloud just below these.

If the current N wave should have started at 9', the idea is similar and possibly a little more dynamic so maybe the price target would be of this type and the 420.00 area would be the extent of the correction. If on the other hand it turned out to be a very dynamic one like so, then for further and for longer.

Figure 5-9: N wave and price target starting at point 9

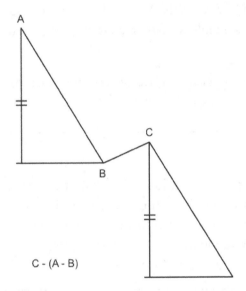

If the whole of the **I wave** which started at 6 and ends at 9' took 66 days, then possibly another I lower of roughly that length of time. Somehow I think this unlikely, but worth keeping in mind when deciding how deep your pockets are and what might be the worst case scenario. This would take us through to early November at worst, and by the beginning of October the Cloud starts moving higher. Note that this would get us beyond potential October jitters. Patience!

Long term

Back to our long-term forecast and using a little bit of Western technical analysis.

From 1955 to 1985 this index languished between 50 and 150, but that does mean it was unable to halve or triple in price. Through to the mid-1990s it consolidated either side of 200, holding between 175 and 250 most of the time. Now you see why gains of 25% are possible.

Triangle consolidation since the middle of last year describes understandable hesitation at all-time highs. The measured target from the triangle is the prediction I gave you earlier, 500 to 540. Getting there should consist of **I waves** interspersed with corrective **N** or **4** waves. We shall have to see how these map out as the Wave Principle is unable to suggest anything longer term than the very next wave.

It is always very difficult when dealing with historic breaks and uncharted territory, so I shall add a massive dollop of caution to all of the above.

Note

I do not make headline-grabbing predictions just to get into the news. Nor am I the doctor of doom, worrying about the end being nigh. The pattern we have on this Dow Jones Utilities Index has been seen over the last couple of years on a number of Asian indices, for example Mumbai's Sensex, Singapore's Straits Times and South Korea's Kospi.

Maybe you would like to consider the economics of this contention. We in the Western world have grown accustomed to cheap gas, electricity, petrol and water. We are the lucky few. Many millions in the third world view these as the best and most elusive of luxuries, and to think they are available on demand – bliss! The Green movement and recent record crude oil prices have made many people a little more aware that basic resources should be used carefully. Higher prices will usually nudge all but the very lazy into thrift.

6

Options Trading
with Clouds

Cloud charts uniquely useful for options trading

THIS CHAPTER IS based on a lecture I gave at the 2002 International Federation of Technical Analysts' conference in London. The theme that year was maximizing profits using technical analysis. Knowing the unique combination of timing and price levels that is possible through Ichimoku Kinko Hyo analysis, I decided to base my talk on options strategies, as options complement very well the time and price elements of the analysis.

One does not have to be a rocket scientist to understand how important price and time are in options strategies – even more so than when trading the underlying instrument. If the expiry date is too early, potential gains may be seriously curtailed or non-existent, as one has not allowed enough time for the move to map out. Choose the wrong strike price, and the market may never get there. Buy an option before an interim high or low is clearly in place and you may suffer a massive drawdown in the value of the option, plus time decay, before things then start moving in the right direction.

Option buyers

The timing element for both buyers and writers of options is very important. Buyers will tend to avoid initiating a trade if it looks likely that prices will move sideways for some time. In a trending market the buyer should analyze the most recent pattern, work out the price target and likely date target, and buy an option with the appropriate strike for expiry just after the day count. For prices that look set to break though Clouds, these should be monitored closely and bought only once they have managed a daily or weekly close through key levels. Be ready to sell an option which has reached its price target sooner than expected in order to recoup some time premium.

Option writers

Those who grant options face a different and difficult task often likened to picking up nickels in front of a bulldozer. Small steady profits can be made by nimble traders, but could be wiped out by one catastrophically big loss. Ideally, all options they sell will expire worthless. Try to sell options which expire just before a cluster of date targets. Also sell options whose strikes are just beyond pattern objectives or big Clouds. If possible concentrate on selling one month options as with these you will know where the Clouds lie, not six month expiries as you won't have the necessary road map.

Let's think in detail about which elements of Ichimoku Kinko charting can help with timing, and which help with price levels.

Time element

For timing, the Time Principle is the obvious place to start. Remember, 9, 17 and 26 days are the basic building blocks, plus combinations of these three. Plot these dates starting at important highs and lows and watch for where these cluster, as this is the most likely date for the next interim high or low. Also consider the Wave Principle, mapping out the most likely path assuming that the next leg will be the same length (or a related number) as the first leg.

Next look at the Cloud itself to see:

- where it thins, and
- whether it crosses over.

These dates are also potentially important turning points. Consider Chikou Span and whether it is struggling among a densely packed group of candles, or whether it is currently soaring or plummeting with no visible signs of resistance or support. In the first case, when in a congestion zone, count how many days forward this continues, say, maybe another three weeks. One would assume therefore that price moves are likely to be limited while this remains the case. In strongly trending markets Chikou Span will not tell you where the move will stop, but it can be useful in determining how far a correction is likely to go as and when prices reverse. In other words, where previous candles will act as support for the current market.

Price levels

Now consider price levels, including objectives, interim support and resistance, and turning points. Again the Price Target Principle is the obvious place to start. Study the size and timing of the previous waves in I, V, N and 4 patterns, then pinpoint the end of the next wave. Adjust this if it lies just the other side of a very big Cloud. Also reduce the price target if, in order to get there, Chikou Span would have to power quickly through a tight cluster of candles.

Conversely, one could increase price targets if the next leg is an I wave and a strong trend already exists. This is also the case when Chikou Span faces no immediate obstacles. Assume very conservative price targets when the moving averages are creeping horizontally across the page.

Trend reversals

How can Ichimoku Kinko charts help in deciding at what price the trend will reverse? When a price target has been met, watch for powerful reversal candles and other conventional signs of topping (basing), for example a double top or rounded bottom. If this also coincides with the edge of a Cloud, so much the better. Similarly, if Chikou Span has hit a brick wall this too will help reverse the trend. Keep in mind support level S, where what had been resistance becomes support and vice versa, as this too is helpful in picking turning points, especially when it coincides with the last leg of a wave pattern.

Support and resistance

Ichimoku Kinko charting helps a lot in terms of interim highs and lows because of its range of staggered support and resistance levels. The moving averages themselves, useful to very active traders, are the first in line - and these also provide support for Chikou Span (remember: it is today's price plotted 26 days ago). The candles of 26 days ago also lend it support/resistance. The top and bottom of the Cloud are usually the next in line to stall a move. Senkou Span B (the highest plus the lowest price of the last 52 days divided by 2) is probably the most important of all, and if prices break decisively through here a very serious re-think, and maybe reversal, of strategy is needed.

The Timespan Principle can also help in picking interim chart levels. For example, in an N wave higher, if the first leg was 17 days long the next one might take nine days. On days seven to eleven when prices are correcting lower, watch carefully for conventional signs that a base is emerging. Once established, one might assume that the final leg higher will take 17 days making it equal to the first impulsive move up. One would end up with a (17+9+17-2) = 41 combination. Again, on days 40 to 44 watch for signs of topping.

Buying option strategies

Long call strategy

This is a good example for a cautious trader who wants to buy an out-of-the-money option. In this example the investor anticipates that the Australian dollar would increase in value versus the US dollar. The chart shows the number of US cents needed to buy one Aussie dollar (the level here is 0.6650, so 66 1/2 US cents). The higher the price, the stronger the Aussie. Believing it should move higher, the trader therefore wants to buy an Aussie call (the same thing as a US dollar put).

Figure 6-1: US dollars per Australian dollar

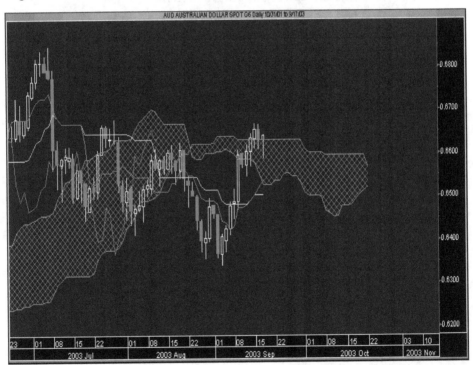

First, check the Cloud and make sure the candlesticks are above the Cloud. If they are not: wait, as a lot of time value may be eroded as prices can stick under the formation for several weeks. Here the Aussie dollar did for almost two months! If they are nudging into the Cloud, and the trader really cannot resist the urge to buy, choose a call with a strike at the top edge of the Cloud and preferably above it (to the nearest round number as these are more actively traded and therefore more keenly priced). Here I would probably look at 0.6600 or 0.6700 calls. As prices break above the top of the Cloud they are likely to start moving quite quickly, increasing implied volatility and thus adding value to the option.

This call can be held until expiry, so long as prices do not break below the bottom of the Cloud. If they trade down below this line, it will probably be worth selling the option in order to recoup some time value and possibly higher implied volatility. Note: as and when prices move higher, so does the Cloud. It continues to provide support as the market rallies and can be used as a trailing stop. Many traders do not think about selling their options, especially in-the-money ones. But if you want increased profitability you should re-assess positions continually to make sure you have the best strategy for current market conditions.

Long put strategy

In this next example, a trader wants to buy a put on the dollar versus the Korean won as the market should hold below the Cloud formation. This one is quoted the European way, as won per US dollar, so the lower we go, the fewer won you need to get yourself a US dollar.

First, make sure the Cloud is thick, rather than the lines crossing over within the next 26 days. Not quite the case here, although they have not crossed, but it is difficult to find perfect examples in current markets, and I always prefer to use up-to-date examples rather than historical ones. So, as this trade assumes the bear trend will continue, the Cloud should be fat to keep this trend heavy and steady.

Next, check that Chikou Span is below the candle of 26 days ago and below the Cloud. Yes, the red line is well below. Buy a put with a strike just below this level, thereby increasing the chance of buying an option that is likely to move into the money quickly.

Figure 6-2: Korean won per US dollar

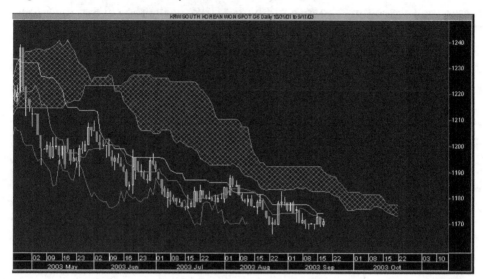

If the trader is correct, then the two Cloud levels should come lower over the life of the option. This time the upper level is used to cut the position to minimize premium losses. Review levels constantly.

A similar, if more elegant strategy when buying options could be achieved with a knock-in which tends to be a lot cheaper than a conventional option. It is an option that only comes into existence when a pre-agreed price level is reached. Premium is paid up front, on the day of purchase, but if the knock-in level is not reached it never becomes a live option. For calls, the knock-in is usually below the current price and well below the strike price; vice versa for a put.

Knock-in strategy

A trader who is bullish on the euro versus the US dollar but the market remains below the Ichimoku Cloud could do the following:

Buy an out-of-the-money call with a strike at the upper edge of the Cloud, say 1.1600. A level below the current price and at the lower edge of the Cloud is used as the knock-in price, say 1.1000. A minimum of one week, more realistically up to one month, should be used for the knock-in period; this for an option that has three months to expiry.

So, the option is very much cheaper than a straight call as the market:

1. may never drop to the knock-in before rallying (which was the case here), or

2. may reach this level after the knock-in period has expired (and so the option never comes into existence).

Figure 6-3: US dollars per euro

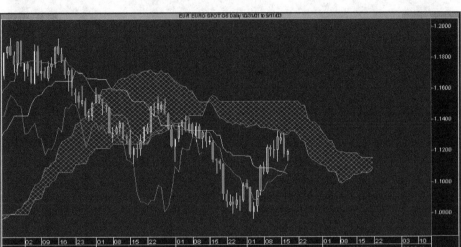

A similar strategy would be a reversal knock in. As we are currently below both levels of the Cloud in the euro example above, the knock-in could be at the lower Cloud level and the strike above the top of the Cloud.

While neat, this strategy would not really save you very much money and certainly not nearly as much as using the standard knock-in described above.

Knock-out option strategy

A knock-out option strategy would again make the option slightly cheaper. This is an option which exists from day one, but then ceases to exist (or dies) if a pre-determined price is touched. For this example I am using sterling versus the US dollar; the lower the price the stronger the dollar.

Figure 6-4: US dollars per pound sterling

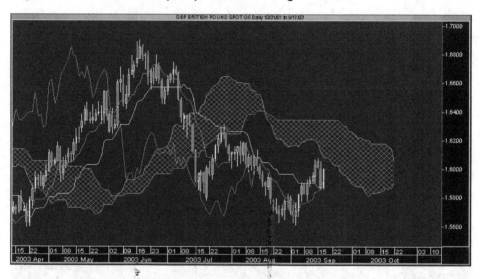

I would suggest the following because the current price is below a decent-sized fat Ichimoku Cloud. Buy an at-the-money put on the pound (a call on the dollar) at 1.6000. Use a level well above the upper edge of the Cloud and above Chikou Span as the knock-out level, say 1.6400. To make money Cable (the USD/GBP rate) would never hit 1.6400 and drop steadily from current prices.

So, if the market went against the trader's strategy (which was the case here), his option would cease to exist as prices break above the top of the Cloud. The most important thing is that the knock-out makes the option cheaper to buy in the first place.

Window knock-out/knock-in strategy

This is my last strategy involving only the purchase of options. This is a Window knock-out/knock-in which capitalizes on the timing aspect of options and Ichimoku Kinko. Windows are options where the knock-in or knock-out elements are shorter than the expiry of the option and are for a pre-selected window of time, say a particular fortnight in the first part of the life of the option. These are even cheaper than straight knock-ins/outs in that not only must the trigger level be hit but it must be hit within the right time frame.

To illustrate this example I shall use the US dollar versus the Japanese yen, again quoted the European way as yen needed to buy one dollar: the higher the price the weaker the yen.

Figure 6-5: Japanese yen per US dollar

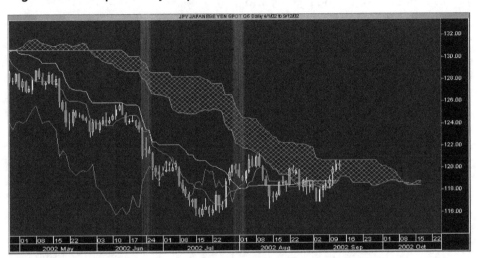

In an ideal world it is nice to see sharp price swings initially, as these would trigger the knock-in (but might just kill it dead as too!), followed by steady moves later on where you don't have to worry about your option unexpectedly expiring on you.

The idea is that, ahead of the Cloud becoming very thin, the investor buys the option assuming that there will be fairly sharp moves at the thin point and eventually a change in trend. Once the new trend has been established, one wants to run the trade and not worry about getting stopped out. In this example I have assumed that we shall be getting some very sharp moves around mid-October, and that we shall eventually get a turn in the long-term trend and that dollar/yen will eventually move up towards 130.00 around year-end.

The key element of this strategy is that we want to buy a three-month dollar call as our long-term view is for a stronger US dollar versus the yen. Say a three-month at-the-money call at 122.00. Why here? This level is above the top of the Cloud and just above August's high at 121.50. Because implied volatility is likely to increase in mid-October, I have taken the view that it is better buy it now rather than wait and have to pay more premium.

The next step is to reduce the cost, which I can do via a knock-in for the two weeks around 10 October - which is the thinnest bit of the Cloud as:

1. you should not be too greedy, and

2. the knock-in is saving such a lot of money that there is some leeway on the choice of trigger price. Above 118.00, so let's settle for 119.00.

As for a knock-out, I think that if dollar/yen broke to a new low for the year, I should probably abandon this whole idea, so let's add a 115.00 knock-out, lasting for the first month of the option. Again, this will reduce the premium I have to pay on day one when I enter into this trade.

Premiums are so much lower with these add-ons, because I am giving away optionality – I am betting against the trend. The cost of this strategy is as follows:

1. For a straight three-month 122.00 the call premium would be 1.8%.

2. The same strategy using a two-week knock-in at 119.00 for the middle two weeks in October reduces the cost of the call to 0.32%.

3. To the above we can add a one-month knock-out (for the first month) at 115.00, reducing the cost of the option yet further, to 0.16%. Less than one tenth of the price of a conventional call, which is not an inconsiderable saving.

Writing option strategies

So far we have just considered strategies that involve buying options, but bankers are more likely to be writing options. This is a bank's natural business; they tend to buy options only to hedge existing positions, to reduce exposure, or as part of a more complex trade.

The first decision when writing a call is where to pitch the strike. Strikes at new highs and new lows tend to be slightly more expensive but, as few Western people know where the Clouds are, we can use these as well as new highs and lows.

Strikes at the top of the Cloud could and should be more expensive, while those within the Cloud can be pitched more cheaply. This is because the market is likely to get stuck inside the Cloud (if it is thick), using up time value. Theta (time decay) is the option seller's friend.

The second decision is when to hedge the call as it moves into-the-money. Let's consider the example below.

Short call strategy

Assume we have sold a C$ 1.4000 call on the US dollar (put on the Canadian dollar). Premium received gives us a cushion, but we should look to start hedging on a daily close above the upper Senkou Span. Once the cushion has been exhausted then these are usually hedged on a sliding scale based on the delta and the expected vega. Also note that this currency pair has been moving broadly sideways in a relatively narrow range since mid-May. Any instrument that is behaving like this is worth considering when granting options as these will hopefully expire worthless, time and time again. Trending markets and those with massive price swings are far more difficult when managing the risk of an options portfolio.

Figure 6-6: Canadian dollars per US dollar

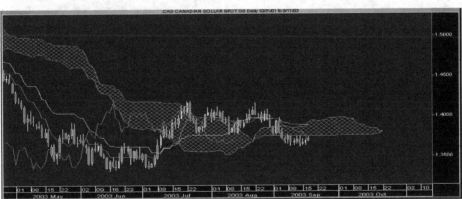

Strangle strategy – making money in a sideways market

Ichimoku is good for trending markets and predicting turns in the trend, but can it be used in sideways markets?

In this example, euro/Swiss franc, we have a market that has been trading broadly sideways for some time and is likely to continue trading in this way as it is neither above or below the Cloud.

Figure 6-7: Swiss francs per euro

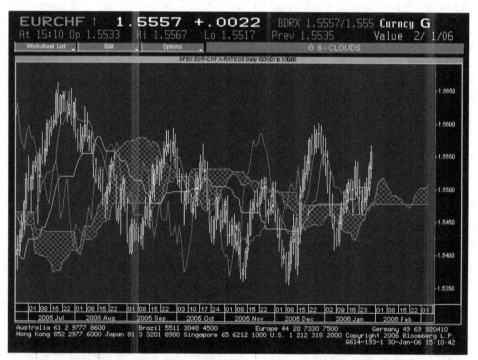

We could sell a straddle (a call and a put with the same expiry date and the same strike) to pick up premium, with the strike at the mean rate of the period: 1.5500 Swiss francs per euro. The option premium received would give us enough cover to allow for several moves around the central rate. Brief moves into the money, either the call or the put, are covered by the option premium received for both legs of the option.

However, based on Ichimoku, I would suggest selling a strangle instead. Pick a call with a strike above the highest Cloud for the period observed (1.5600) and a put with a strike below the lowest Chikou Span level (1.5350). The premium received would be a lot less than a straightforward straddle, but I think that running the position would be less stressful. Time value will steadily erode until the option expires worthless. Premium income equals net gain to the writer.

Note that these types of strategies are used a lot in the interbank market, and participants will go to great lengths to protect the options they have sold so as to ensure they expire worthless.

Note

As a rule of thumb, in FX circles we like to:

• write **plain vanilla** options (simple basic strategies) in *low volatility* environments, and

• write **exotics** (option strategies with all the ding-dongs) in *high volatility* situations.

This saves the writer money when the market is flying about as knock-outs are more likely to be triggered, making options worthless.

Double-no-touch strategy – sideways markets

Another strategy for a market that is likely to go nowhere over the next month or so would be a double-no-touch.

A double-no-touch means that the options remain alive so long as neither a pre-established upper or lower level trade. The writer of the strategy should chose touch levels that are far enough away to satisfy the buyer, but preferably inside the Cloud or recent high/low points.

So for EUR/CHF (Figure 6-7) I would try to sell a double-no-touch with an upper level at last summer's high (1.5650) and a lower level at 1.5350. With a little luck these levels are likely to be hit, again killing the option leaving the writer with the premium and no position to worry about.

Selling a call spread

As can be seen in the chart below, prices are just below a nice fat Cloud and the trader thinks they will hold below here and move lower again. However, the Cloud structure has deteriorated so there is a chance that we might break higher in October.

I would suggest selling an at-the-money call and buying a second, out-of-the-money call, for the same expiry - a strategy known as a call spread. Premium received will be more than that paid out, making this a good way to work with Clouds. The call you sell will be in the middle of the Cloud. The premium received should be more than enough to cover you until the top of the Cloud, the strike of the second call you are buying. The market gets stuck in the middle; time wasted and you have made a profit. But, if the trend really does change, then one-for-one the option you bought will cover the losses on the option you granted.

Figure 6-8: Singapore dollars per US dollar

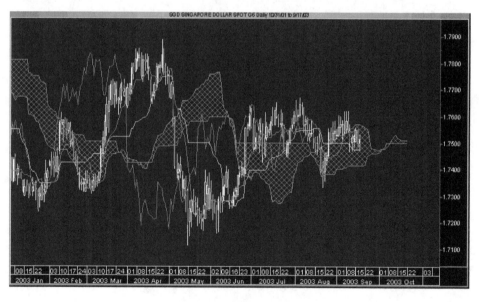

Variations on this idea could include buying twice as many out-of-the-money calls. This would, of course, be more expensive; to be able to do this the Cloud would have to be a lot thicker (and the strike prices further away from each other, so that the premium paid equals premium received). In this case, if the market breaks higher, then the first out-of-the-money call bought covers the losses on the call granted. The second way out-of-the-money call bought makes money as a speculative position.

Selling a calendar spread

Here, instead of using nice fat Clouds, we are looking to the point at which the Senkou Span lines cross. For this example we'll look at the Swedish krona against the Norwegian krone (quoted as Swedish units needed to buy one Norwegian one).

Figure 6-9: Swedish krona per Norwegian krone

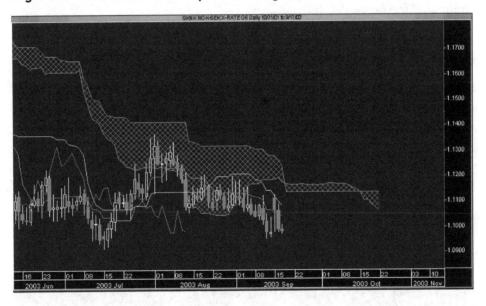

In late August and September, the market pushes up against the Cloud and pulls back. The Cloud is expected to halt further rallies, but not forever. The thinness suggests a break higher by the end of October.

Strategy: sell a three-week call using the top of the Cloud as the strike, 1.1200. This option will hopefully expire worthless, as the market will not have broken higher by then. Timing is obviously key here, with the choice of strike a secondary issue. Premium received can be used to fund part of another call at the same strike, or all of a call at a higher strike. But this second option starts two/three weeks later and expires two/three weeks after the first one. To make it more affordable it could also have a knock-in (say at 1.0950) before it comes into existence.

Another idea for a market that has very fat Clouds with a thin bit in the middle and where you anticipate that the market will change direction, is a box trade. Buy a call at the top of the Cloud (1.1200 again). Fund it by selling a put below Chikou Span (1.0900). The premium on the two should be roughly equal.

Selling a butterfly spread

A more complex variation on the preceding strategy would be selling a butterfly spread. For this example I will use the Hungarian forint against the US dollar (quoted as forints to the dollar).

Figure 6-10: Hungarian Forints per euro

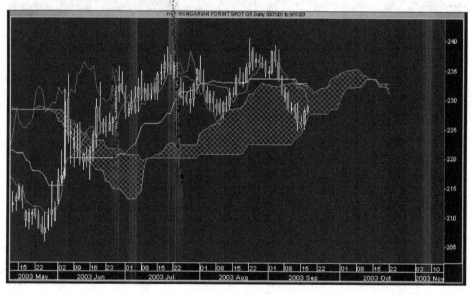

The Clouds are not as fat as I would have liked. Anyway, we will sell a 230.00 call, buy two 232.50 calls, and then sell a 235.00 call to help fund this little gem. All for the same maturity. This trade is market bullish and volatility bullish, with positive delta and gamma. The two 232.50 calls will cover any losses on the first call sold and, with a little luck, the other call sold will expire before moving into the money.

Conclusion

Most option strategies revolve around trading bands, trends and timing. Ichimoku Kinko captures all these ideas in a very graphic and immediate way.

But more importantly, option trading requires even more thought and attention than outright positioning. All too often investors become tremendously complacent: buying an option because the risk is perceived to be lower, or happily hanging on to the option, especially if it is in-the-money, not realizing they may now hold an outright position or an inefficient strategy. Trading is something to be approached fresh every day, with an open mind and a sensible, flexible strategy.

Recommendations

- Every day check the trend and whether the original view is still correct.
- Check implied volatility and, if it is ridiculously high, consider selling out the option.
- Understand whether you want a high or low delta.
- Time decay, which accelerates dramatically in the last few days in the life of an option, can be used to your advantage.

Option trading is not easy, but Ichimoku Kinko Clouds can help enhance your returns.

7

An Update on How I Use Cloud Charts Today

In this chapter I aim to update you on how, over the last ten years, I have used what Bloomberg call *General Overview Charts*, how I have adapted them to my needs, and what I have chucked out along the way. Obviously I have learnt a lot – and not just about Clouds. Hopefully, I'm also wiser, as well as older – and a better writer too! I'm also proud to say that I am possibly one of a very select few Gaijin (Westerners) who have used this Japanese method of charting for over twenty years – on top of the previous fifteen using Classic Dow Theory.

Why I like Ichimoku

I look back and wonder why I started researching the Cloud charting system. The answer is easy and it's got to do with my favourite quote, which is from Eleanor Roosevelt:

> I think, that at a child's birth, if a mother could ask a fairy godmother to endow it with the most useful gift, that gift would be curiosity.

I am constantly, and unconsciously, curious. I love the thrill of the new, keeping my eyes wide open and my thinking fresh. I read extensively, and not just technical analysis! Poetry, biography, scientific, and economic journals – then ditching much of it. Never matter. Avoid conventional media which tends to repeat itself thereby reinforcing conventional wisdom, now labelled the echo chamber. In fact, one of the most successful professional traders I have known didn't come to the office, preferring to work alone at home. He wanted to prevent his thinking becoming tainted by prevailing standard views. He'd say, "watch out, experts about!"

I was attracted to Ichimoku because I could see that it clearly brought new ideas to the charts and seemed intuitively to work. The Clouds are easy to understand and very visual, so I'm not in the least bit surprised that they have been embraced all over the world. Simply, the Clouds work, though not without serious limitations. First and most important is that it is a trending method which, as we all know, is a killer when markets are in consolidation phases. Stemming from that, the single most important decision when using any moving average method is: are we trending or not? (Not on Twitter, of course!) Though one can never be sure until well after the event, markets do trend often, but certainly not all of the time. Depending on the instrument, my rule of thumb is somewhere between 30% and 70% of the time can we look forward to trends. Only a handful of very mature instruments with a lot of volume tend to keep in defined ranges for several years (such as Citicorp – see the following chart).

Figure 7-1: Citicorp (2009–2017)

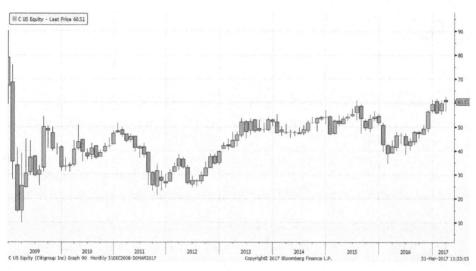

Trends tend to alternate, not just from bull to bear and vice versa, but long term versus short waves, and big price runs versus brief ones. Therefore if you've just lived through a strong bull run, there is a greater chance that it will be reversed rather than just cling to current prices. The reversal, however, is likely to be shorter in time and magnitude than the previous move. On the other hand, if you've been slinking along the bottom of the chart for all too long, it will take a really big energy boost or surprise jolt to lift it out of its torpor.

Keeping these ideas at the fore forces my thinking to be more objective when ticking off each item of Ichimoku when a price is in the process of reversing. Whether the Cloud or the moving averages give way first is irrelevant (though chances are it'll be the averages); what matters is that they all are singing from the same hymn sheet and my confidence grows as, one at a time, they fall into place. It's not a bolt out of the blue but an incremental change in tactics. It provides multiple entry and exit warning levels and is not an all-or-nothing system like so many oscillators.

Manic markets must be treated differently and happen a lot more often than you'd think; the famous black swan of Nassim Taleb is more of a flock than a singular bird.

Moving averages lag badly and therefore the Cloud does so even more as, though plotted ahead of time, its maths lags because it's based on past prices. I would suggest ditching all of these and focusing on the candles alone, either individual reversal ones (Shooting Star), pairs (Tweezers and Bearish Engulfing) and trios (Evening Stars and Islands). Or, looking for a reversal pattern, the shapes a handful of these might make. Obviously a top is likely to form faster than a base and lengthy rounded reversals and so on are more often found at lows.

Which brings me to the use of the mid-point to calculate the nine and twenty-six day moving averages. The more I think of it, the more it makes sense, especially in markets which are not exchange-traded or have extended opening hours. This is increasingly the case, not only with foreign exchange which has always been a 24-hour market, but now futures, options and stocks which have after-hours trading. With these a 'closing price' is an arbitrary concept. The question of what is a trading day also crops up, and the answer to this can also only be arbitrary. I tend to use the Far East opening price as the start of the trading day, with the New York close bookending it, Monday to Friday. This means that my morning is roughly 20:00 pm GMT the night before, something some chart packages plot separately on Sundays, so that the trading week has six 'days'. Can you imagine the mess this makes of all your averages! It is also worth noting that the Middle East starts its week with Sunday trading (and is closed on Fridays and Saturdays).

From here you get to the real nub of the matter: data. This goes deeper than whether your software provider is any good. I've seen so many packages that use the wrong formulas, that plot things incorrectly, that are quite frankly dangerous. So, before signing up to a data service, give them a really good grilling – something you'll only be able to do if you know your subject well. Then investigate where their feeds come from. Exchange-traded are the easiest to verify. Over the counter a nightmare more often than not. The in-betweens, for example trading platforms that mirror prices on exchanges, a tricky proposition. Then: is the data clean? Have incorrect trades been deleted? Are 'fat fingers' regularly eliminated? Imagine what will happen to Senkou Span B if a rogue high or low sits in the data for 52 hours, days or weeks. Rubbish charts, of course.

Timing

I've always realised that timing the market gives you the biggest edge. As do fund managers' adverts, which all too often proclaim, 'if you'd invested £10,000 in year X' – where X is a key low. While unlikely to pick the absolute low, Ichimoku and its series of rules that kick-in will confirm a new trend. It also gives you staying power for the medium to long term. It stops you getting shaken out when the market stalls or by intermediate corrections. Herein lies its strength, as can be seen by how well it has worked with stock indices since 2009. In fact, I think the popularity of the technique can be largely credited to its performance here. Likewise, at highs and deciding whether to get out. It's also a phased process and does not have the speedy decisions that reversal candles can help you with.

Figure 7-2: S&P 500 (2009–2017)

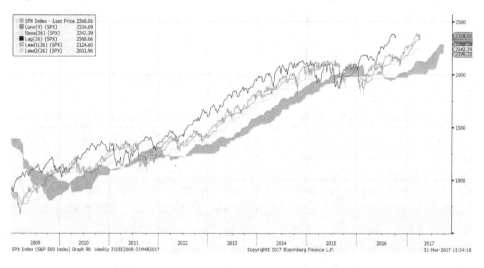

Here we can see that the weekly Ichimoku Cloud managed to stem intermediate corrections to this very long bull run. A bit of slippage in 2011 and 2016, but fairly quickly one would have seen that the market was still in positive mode.

Figure 7-3: FTSE 100 (2009–2017)

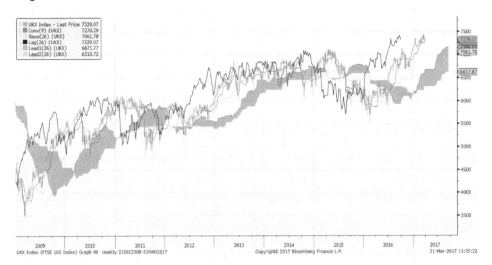

Lagging Line

I have issues with the Lagging Line. Sometimes I like it and sometimes I choose to ignore it. If I think it's probably irrelevant (at best) or a hindrance (at worst), I tend to change its colour to white (so it blends in to a white background), though the keen-eyed can still see its shadow as it creeps through the Cloud.

When I follow it, it must earn its keep. It comes into its own in seriously trending markets and you're worried just how far a correction might go. You look back at the candles of 26 days or weeks ago and see where support or resistance levels might start to appear.

Talking of background colour: I use white because printing the chart doesn't use nearly as much toner. I have used a series of different coloured charts in this book to help you decide which combination might be the one you prefer.

Price targets

The Wave counts are a pain in the neck. Or maybe that's just me, as I've also struggled for years with Elliott Wave – despite my name! I love price targets though. To me they are something I've always used and I base mine on chart patterns, the size of the waves, and Fibonacci numbers. A rally of 61, 100 or 161% is totally doable; bigger ones like 261% at a push. When these targets align with Fibonacci retracements or trend lines, so much the better. Just as targets from well-known patterns like head-and-shoulders are used and quoted all the time, if these line up with price targets, so much the better. The more technical analysis levels you have clustering in any one area, the more likely it is to be seriously important – if only because many traders, and not just a few, have their eye on it.

Sustainability

The Timespan Principle has merit – and backs up those who like Tom De Mark and the Rule of Eight (to Ten). Cycle theory also, Fibonacci or otherwise, posits that changes in trend occur at regular intervals. And economists believe in time cycles that can be observed, and which underpin, economic growth. All of these suggest that any market which has moved in just one direction for between eight and ten consecutive hours/days/weeks/months/years has seen a mature move and is due a correction. Underlining all these similar ideas is the concept of sustainability. Have we over-egged the pudding and are we becoming just too greedy? The natural ebb and flow of markets, water, and moods is a universal concept.

Being a contrarian

When I started, some aspects of Ichimoku Clouds were considered contrarian thinking. Though Cloud charts have not been embraced by all and sundry, no longer can they be classified as alternative. So they inhabit a half-way house between mainstream and far out; this matters. It's lonely and difficult being a contrarian and the herding instinct is strong. But from my experience conventional thinking is usually wrong because anyone with money has already put on that trade and there's no one left to join in. In other words, zero momentum. The Clouds, and technical analysis generally, keep you anchored and helps distance emotion from investment decisions.

Like the perennial favourite: interest rates can only go up and back to 'normal'. Still waiting here.

Figure 7-4: US 10-year Treasury yield (2009–2017)

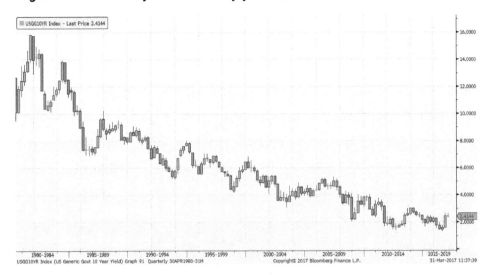

It's worth remembering that the field of technical analysis does not suit everyone's thinking. That is because we have been schooled in a different way, have a natural flair for some subjects rather than others, and we might lean towards the methodical and structured ways of thinking while others are creative types.

I would posit that Ichimoku Cloud charts are a good mix between the two. Attention to detail in the shape of the candles, plus flair to see how they build into patterns that are so often imperfect. Similarly the rigour of the five lines and the Three Principles, with the confidence of knowing that one is in trending mode. In a way it's akin to using chart patterns with just one oscillator: vision and rigour.

Recently some are suggesting that Asian people tend to enjoy and grasp technical analysis, including Ichimoku Cloud charts, better than others. While initially sounding a little racist maybe, it does go to the heart of the formulaic and rote learning that is common in Asian schools. It's perhaps also testament to the importance parents put on learning and getting the right qualifications forcing their kids into hours of homework. What cannot be denied is that the Japanese were probably the first to use charts for wholesale trading.

8

New Case Study

Blind analysis

I AM USING Bloomberg charts in this chapter because they are one of the few systems where I can set start and end dates on charts. This means that the lines will end at the day I've chosen, so we can see a snapshot of exactly what would've been there on the specific day. To ensure that I'm not fudging the issue, all daily charts start on the first working day in January, as do weekly ones, going through to end-December.

I have deliberately chosen an instrument you may not know; this is so that you will approach this chapter with no pre-conceived ideas of what you should be looking for or what you thought at that point in time. Say I had chosen the S&P 500 in early 2008, well, you'd probably bring a whole load of baggage along with you.

As an aside here, I would urge you all to, on a regular basis, open up a chart you have never, ever seen before – the world of individual shares is a ripe seam to mine here. Look carefully, and analyse it in a professional technical way. Don't just brush it aside as an irrelevance, but start from scratch doing the sort of rigorous, non-judgmental analysis we should all be doing all of the time – but often don't!

Now I want you to focus only on the candles and the Ichimoku Cloud chart system; who cares what the market is (but trust me, because this is clean, exchange-traded data). We'll work through time frames and please remember, like all charting, you and I may not come to the same conclusions. Look at the charts first and decide how you might approach this market; make notes you can refer back to. Then see my comments and compare with your ideas. Remember, there is no right or wrong way to go about it. Differences will always pop up in any area of learning.

First decide whether this market is currently trending; really trending, and if so, is it a strong trend? Look at the vertical scale and calculate the percentage price move between highest and lowest points. Is it statistically significant? Paraphrasing: is it worth getting out of bed for? If it's not trending, what would you suggest?

Let's get cracking.

We're going to work through a series of daily and weekly charts starting in 2011. It's very important to work with different time frames, tabbing between them, different time horizons and history, to take a careful look at the candles themselves; are they fractals of each other? Then to look at the small patterns and how they fit into the bigger one. To see how the oscillators may diverge dramatically between time horizons; to decide when evasive action is essential and when it's right to take a more relaxed attitude.

Here's the first chart.

Figure 8-1

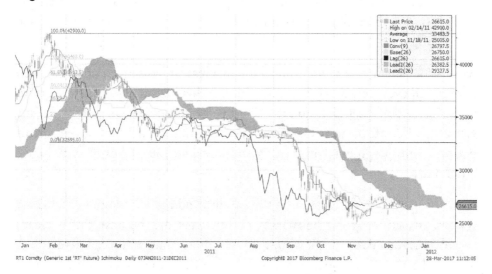

RT1 Comdty (Generic 1st 'RT' Future) Ichimoku Daily 07JAN2011-31DEC2011   Copyright© 2017 Bloomberg Finance L.P.   28-Mar-2017 11:12:05

I can tell you that in January 2011 this market had been in a very strong uptrend for some years. In fact, it had almost quintupled in price from a long-term base in December 2008. You can see that it's been holding above the 9 and 26-day moving averages, well above the top of a rising Cloud. However, after trading higher for nine consecutive days twice during January alone, the Timespan Principle would have set off warning signs that the market was overheated.

A head and shoulders little top through to the end of February saw moving averages cross to bearish on the daily close below a rather crooked neckline. A break below horizontal support at 38600 sees it slump through the sharply rising thick Cloud (a surprise to me anyway) – another bearish sign.

March stages a dramatic comeback but the Cloud caps – even when it is terribly thin mid-April, suggesting bearish pressure might be stronger than one would imagine. The bounce is also capped at Fibonacci 61.8% retracement resistance from February's increasingly important high. Then down we go, the Cloud consistently grinding prices lower through to the end of the year.

Note that moving averages proved unreliable between May through to September, as one would expect, when the drift has been so very slow.

Now we're looking forward to next year in a bearish frame of mind as prices bump against the bottom of the Cloud in December 2011.

Figure 8-2

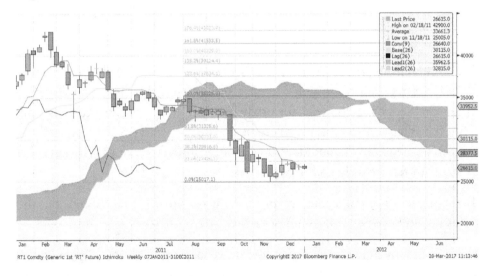

Another year, 2012, so let's start with a weekly chart since January 2011 to date. Clearly bearish, but rather a long way below the fat, steady, very horizontal Cloud, capped neatly by the nine-week moving average though. Since February the drop was a three wave move, where the last one was 140% the size of the first (which is not a Fibonacci projection, just any old number), and since October we have consolidated in potential 5 wave narrowing triangle according to the Wave Principle. The bear trend is intact on all counts.

Figure 8-3

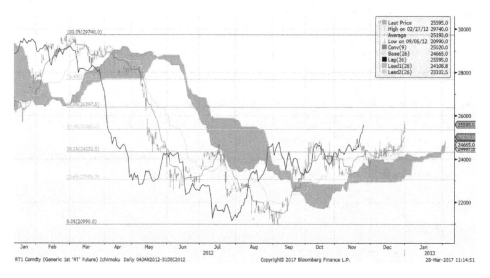

RT1 Comdty (Generic 1st 'RT' Future) Ichimoku Daily 04JAN2012-31DEC2012   Copyright© 2017 Bloomberg Finance L.P.   28-Mar-2017 11:14:51

The daily chart in January 2012 comes as a massive surprise. A sharp rally from 26000 to almost 30000, which will have shaken even the most complacent. I mean, that's a 20% rally we'd not predicted from either of our previous time frames. But remember, 30115 is where the 26-week moving average lies and the bottom of the weekly Cloud doesn't even start until 32500 or so. The rally also manages to retrace only half of September-November's drop.

Therefore, let's not panic and accept that this is a volatile market and that the bear's nerves have been shaken, not rattled.

Sure enough, by mid-March daily moving averages turned bearish again and in a neat step we drop to the bottom of the Cloud – the breaking of which kicks off a major slump. From 28000 to 23000 by early June – another 20% or so – underlining the fact we should prepare for this sort of thing with this market.

Interestingly in this drop we never see nine or more consecutive daily declines, so the Timespan Principle would not have set off any alarm bells. So, if price action from mid-November 2011 to early May 2012 is a rectangle, then its first measured target (based on its height) is approximately 20500 – which it nearly got to but just missed. By September things start getting sluggish and messy. The daily chart provided a great, neat, short-term buying opportunity mid-

September to capture a small rally, retracing exactly a Fibonacci 61.8% of the drop since March. One for nimble professionals.

Figure 8-4

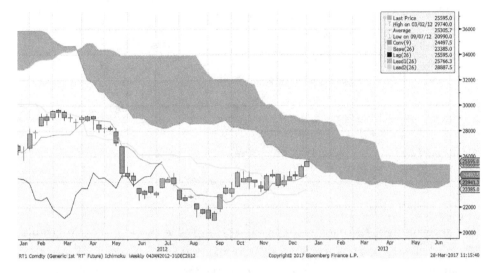

December 2012 ends on a bullish short term note but looking at the weekly chart, we can see that while the nine-week moving average has edged prices higher they've just hit the bottom of a large, relentless, descending, fat weekly Cloud.

Fat chance!

It really does look ominous and a tough nut to crack for a little bull.

Figure 8-5

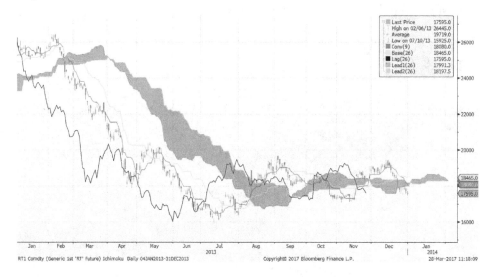

Last Price	17595.0
High on 02/06/13	26445.0
Average	19719.0
Low on 07/10/13	15925.0
Conv(9)	18080.0
Base(26)	18465.0
Lag(26)	17595.0
Lead1(26)	17991.3
Lead2(26)	18197.5

RT1 Comdty (Generic 1st 'RT' Future) Ichimoku Daily 04JAN2013-31DEC2013   Copyright© 2017 Bloomberg Finance L.P.   28-Mar-2017 11:18:09

And sure enough, the daily chart in 2013 struggles with a double top around 26300, then sees nothing but a steady, serious decline from 26000 to 16000 by mid-July, despite (and worrying for long-term bears) nine consecutive weekly decline from March to April. From then on, once again things become more sluggish – feeling all too familiar to the second half of 2012 – even more like a patient etherised upon a table.

Again, let's ignore and switch to a weekly chart – while considering whether there's something seasonal about this market. Perhaps we've witnessed another five Wave Principle move in a narrowing triangle.

Figure 8-6

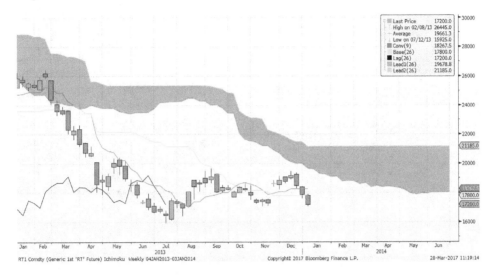

December 2013 ends on a bearish weekly note as we remain clearly below the bottom of the weekly Cloud and, while moving averages are a bit of a mess as one would expect in a sideways move around 18000 they have now turned bearish on the daily chart and prices have dropped below the bottom of the Cloud.

Remember that there is also a potential double top in the second half of 2013 around 19500. And what about the three black crows?

Are you beginning to understand the thinking behind my switching between time frames, techniques, and strategies?

You can do this too with your own choices of oscillators or whatever.

Figure 8-7

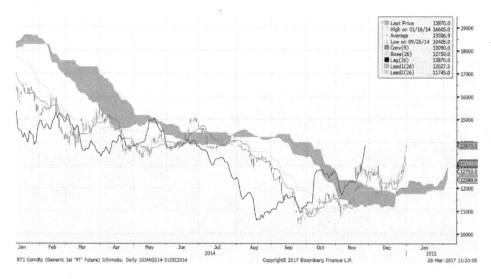

So, January 2014, and here we go again.

Down, down, deeper and down, with a bit of a glitch mid-June as prices move sideways around 14000.

Seasonality kicking in again?

Or perhaps just a market of two halves. It's clear that prices are settling down at these lower levels and that it is happier than it was around 40000 plus. Breaking lower again in August for a drop to levels not seen since roughly December 2008.

One must ask oneself: is this starting to look seriously cheap?

In November 2014 things become less predictable. Trading at a quarter of 2011's peak, what shall we do? We've seen a three wave rally through the daily Cloud, in fact gapping above it, and moving averages have turned bullish. It's quite perky managing in just eight working weeks to put on almost 3000 points – from 11000 to 14000. Again, a hefty 27% rise. Hello!

Figure 8-8

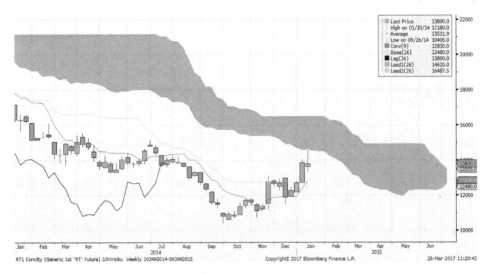

RT1 Comdty (Generic 1st 'RT' Future) Ichimoku Weekly 10JAN2014-09JAN2015   Copyright® 2017 Bloomberg Finance L.P.   28-Mar-2017 11:20:43

Yet again we flip to a weekly chart in January 2015 so that we can look back at the year that was; keeping in mind the nifty little rally late last year. And lo! Though weekly moving averages have just turned bullish, we have a Shooting Star candle under the bottom of a determinedly bearish weekly Cloud; this is really oppressive and exactly the sort of stuff that wears one down. The blip above 14000 looks like a proper false break and the lagging line is getting snagged in the candles of 26 weeks ago. This still looks very bearish long term.

Figure 8-9

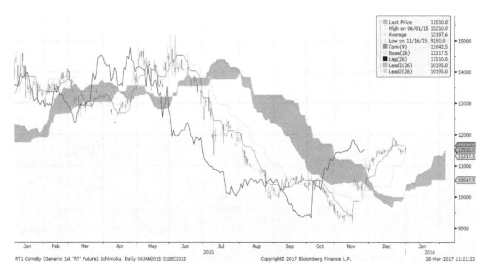

Another year and can things still be so bearish?

This is what they call a long term, if not a secular, bear market and is a lesson to all who hope for quick turnarounds. Once again, we turn to a daily chart for 2015. A sideways mess in the first half of the year, trading roughly in a rectangle between 13000 and 14500 – a much narrower range than at the highs in 2011. Keep both height and width in mind in case of a break to calculate price targets.

A change in tone in that, in previous years, when the first six months were seriously bearish and then snaked sideways. Is this a turn up for the books? July reverts to a serious bear, losing another 38% of face value into November, managing 100% of the measured target based on the width of the rectangle (bigger than the height).

Ouch!

This market, which when we started looking at it was worth over 40000, is now worth a fraction of that: it's probably time to start thinking it might be seriously cheap.

The drop to 9150, nearly the psychological 9000, is a five wave move starting at 15200, and where C is just over 100% of A; more Elliott Wave than price target, but related anyway. Then gapping seriously higher mid-November causing moving averages to cross quickly and not in the sluggish way they have done previously. Prices burst smartly through a thin, descending Cloud. Antennae picking up to a change in tone; not sure yet though as bearishness has become ingrained in the psyche towards this market. The 9-day moving average is zooming higher and the 26-day one is holding the low on the last day in December.

Can it do its job? Will it bring in better times?

Figure 8-10

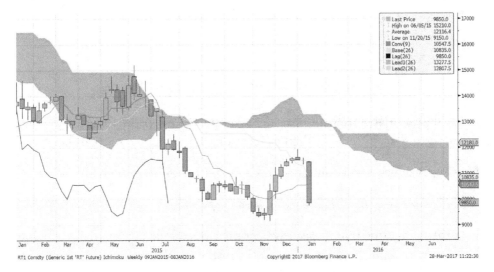

Oh dear!

January 2016 is a disaster and not what we had hoped. All elements of the weekly Ichimoku chart are still bearish. Just too depressing for words and why wouldn't anyone involved in this market throw in the towel and give up all positive hope.

Figure 8-11

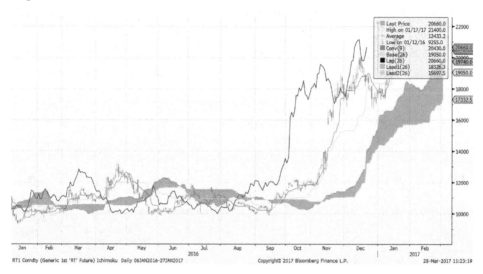

Then, it grips desperately for dear life to support at the psychological 10000 in February and again in May, then months on end through to September.

No proper rallies mind you, but not giving up the ghost either.

Will it? Won't it? Can it reverse half a decade of decay?

In a tiny range for ten consecutive months (rectangle again?) daily moving averages turn bullish late September, but only in November do things look fractionally more positive with the break above 12000. Prices then perform a massive gap, and no wonder, as they break above 14000 – which had been resistance for nearly all of the time since 2014.

At last!

A serious, stonking rally that looks and feels like something too many may had hoped for, for too long. The daily chart, with V-shaped consolidation around 18000, looks positive.

Figure 8-12

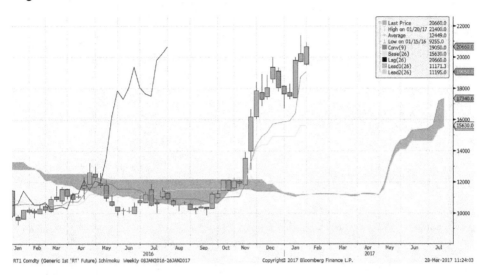

Daily and weekly charts in January 2017 look as though we might have seen the first leg in a series of bullish moves that we can look forward to for the rest of this year. We have currently retraced exactly a Fibonacci 38.2% of declines since 2011. Good, strong stuff for what might be the first in a series of bullish waves starting at very cheap levels.

Remember though, one day at a time.

A final chart to recap: daily since 2011 (and therefore rather tiny). The change in tone between Q3 2015 and Q3 2016 is palpable.

For those of you who want to know, this was the chart of the front month contract of rubber on the Shanghai futures exchange, a derivative that has been listed and actively traded since 1996 and is priced in yuan per metric tonne.

Figure 8-13

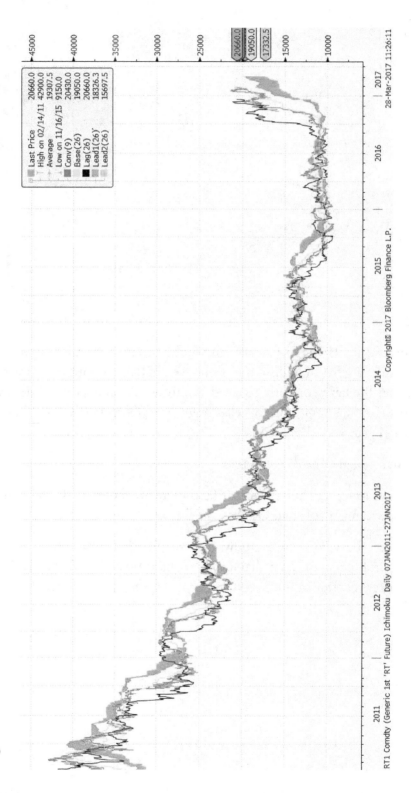

Conclusion

LOOKING BACK ON what I wrote a decade ago, and what I have added this year, I am amazed that the book has survived the test of time, and I am pleased that so many have added Ichimoku Cloud charts to their tool box. Mainly professional technical analysts, but also amateurs and those who dabble in the subject for the sheer pleasure of doing so. And I think that is at the heart of the method's popularity. It is very visual; it is fairly straightforward, and above all, it works!

The principles of Cloud charts are at the heart of charts – all sorts of charts. They simplify and emphasise the salient features of a data set. They can, of course, be used to highlight certain desired – and undesirable – features of trends, from demographics, to inflation, to financial markets. Therefore I am not in the least bit surprised at the increased use of infographics in the press, both print and online.

Years ago my nephew, nieces, godchildren, and other kids used to ask me what I did in my work day. As a firm believer in explaining to them about work, I invited them to come and see my office and computers. I organised outings to TV studios and news bureaux, and I'd show them some charts. Usually tangible things, like the price of gold, lean hogs, or wheat. Being little Europeans, they were also happy with the exchange rate between pound and the euro or the US dollar! And I'd casually mention that we were looking for patterns – and list a number of potential ones that we might find. And just like that, they'd dive in, spotting rounded bottoms, triangles and rectangles. From there, we'd move to trend lines – which they'd be encouraged to draw (in pencil so there was no fear of getting it wrong and they could rub it out) and within 45 minutes they'd got it. The sparkle in their eyes and pride in doing 'real work' was all the encouragement I needed.

Finally, a little bit of poetry and something for my older readers. 'Both Sides, Now' is one of Joni Mitchell's best-known songs. First recorded by Judy Collins in 1967, it subsequently appeared on Mitchell's 1969 album *Clouds*. She re-recorded the song in a lusher, orchestrated version for her 2000 album *Both Sides Now*; this version was subsequently featured on the soundtrack to the 2003 film *Love Actually*. So says Wikipedia – and who am I to quibble?

Both Sides, Now

Rows and flows of angel hair
And ice cream castles in the air
And feather canyons everywhere,
I've looked at clouds that way.

But now they only block the sun,
They rain and snow on everyone
So many things I would have done,
But clouds got in my way.

I've looked at clouds from both sides now
From up and down and still somehow
It's cloud illusions I recall
I really don't know clouds at all

Moons and Junes and Ferris wheels,
The dizzy dancing way you feel
As every fairy tale comes real,
Oh, I've looked at love that way.

But now it's just another show,
You leave 'em laughing when you go
And if you care, don't let them know,
Oh, don't give yourself away.

I've looked at love from both sides now
From give and take and still somehow

It's love's illusions I recall
Oh, I really don't know love at all

Tears and fears and feeling proud,
To say "I love you" right out loud
Dreams and schemes and circus crowds,
I've looked at life that way.

But now old friends they're acting strange,
They shake their heads, they say I've changed
Well something's lost, but something's gained
In living every day.

I've looked at life from both sides now
From win and lose and still somehow
It's life's illusions I recall
Oh, I really don't know life at all

Appendix

Constructing candlestick charts

Candlesticks are similar to bar charts. For any given period, say a month, a day or an hour, prices are plotted vertically on a chart moving from left to right by the chosen time interval. The examples used here will be days, but the rules apply equally to all other periods. A note is made of the opening price, the high and low points, and the closing price that day. The high and low are treated in the conventional way, joined with a vertical line, but the other two points are configured differently than in a bar chart. The open and close are used to form the real body of the candle and are plotted as a slightly wider section around the vertical line. The vertical line that extends above the real body is called the upper shadow, while the line extending below it is known as the lower shadow. On bar charts the open is sometimes plotted as a small horizontal line to the left of the bar, while the close is always plotted as a small horizontal line to the right. If these were joined, you can see it is only a small step from bars to candles.

Figure A-1: Open and close

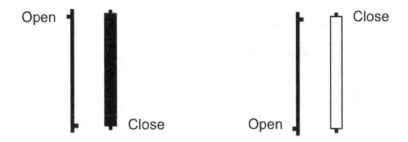

If prices open high and trade down towards the close, the body of the candle is coloured in black (or any other of the six million colours available on today's computers). If the market closes above where it opened, then the body is left empty – traditionally white, based upon the use of white graph paper.

Figure A-2: Doji patterns

Patterns formed by the candlesticks are given a name when they signal a possible change in the prevailing trend. One of the most common of these is a Doji – derived from the Japanese for 'simultaneous' – which occurs when the open and close are at exactly the same level and the body is represented by a small horizontal line.

A Gravestone Doji is one that looks like the letter T, with the opening and closing prices at the same level and at one extreme of the day's price range. It looks like an inverted T when the open and the close are at the low of the day.

The three key elements to study are:

1. total day's range, and how this lies relative to the body,

2. the colour of the body, and

3. the body size relative to the whole candlestick

Figure A-3: Spinning Tops and Bottoms

Big bodies logically mean that the market has seen a sizeable move in price that day. The closer the open and close are to the extremes of the day's range, the bigger the body, and the more momentum in the market. Conversely, the smaller the body, the more evenly matched are buyers and sellers, and the higher the likelihood of a trend reversal. Small bodies with shadows of equal size at either end are called spinning tops or spinning bottoms depending on where they lie at the end of a trend.

Figures A-4 and A-5: Shooting Star or Hanging Man, and a Hammer

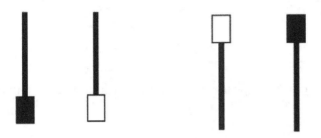

A very reliable pattern is one that has a small body (of either colour) at one end of a large daily range, showing that a market has opened and scurried all the way to the other extreme, only to reverse direction and finish back where it started. At the top of a bull trend this formation is called a Shooting Star or Hanging Man; at the bottom of a bear trend it's called a Hammer, as the pattern looks like a mallet. These are considered very powerful and clear chart signals that warn of an immediate and often violent change in trend.

Figure A-6: Bullish Engulfing

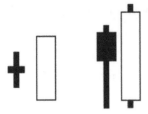

Other reversal patterns look at two or more candles in succession. A Bullish Engulfing pattern is one where, on day two, there is a candle with a large white body whose range is bigger than the previous day's real body. Ideally a doji occurs on the first day, followed by a candle whose body is bigger than the whole of the previous day's range.

Figure A-7: Bearish Engulfing

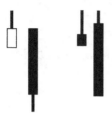

A Bearish Engulfing pair is the opposite, with a large black body eclipsing the previous small body.

Figure A-8: Dark Cloud Cover

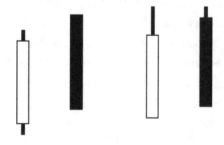

Dark Cloud Cover is a similar topping pattern, but the second day's black body does not totally eclipse the previous day's white body, which can be as big as day two's body.

Figure A-9: Piercing pattern

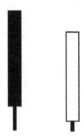

Piercing pattern is its name at the bottom of a trend when a large white candle does not quite overlap the previous day's black one.

Figure A-10: Harami

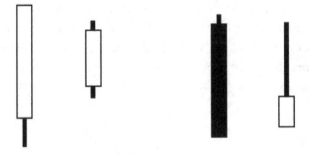

Harami (stemming from the Japanese word for pregnant) are patterns that are also made up of two days' worth of candles, where the second day's body (which can be either colour) lies totally within the previous day's big body. These are the opposite of the engulfing patterns and what we Western chartists would call an inside day. These patterns denote uncertainty, and show that a potential turning point in that the big day's move has seen no follow-through.

Figure A-11: Evening Star

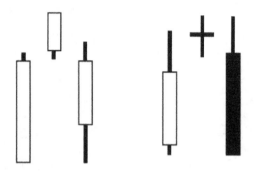

Three black crows (three consecutive big black bodies) at the top of a bull trend are, as the name hints, an evil omen and suggest the trend will turn down.

Three white soldiers at the bottom of a bear market are the opposite and hint at a bullish trend emerging. Other three-candle combinations are the morning and evening stars with the former at a bottom and the latter at a top. The first candle in a evening star combo has a large white body; the second day's small body does not touch the first body, nor does it touch the third day's big black body. Similar in idea to an island top.

Figure A-12: Morning Star

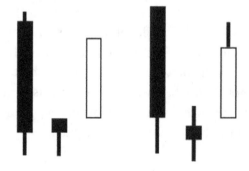

The reverse holds for a Morning Star where the third candle is white and the first one has a big black body. The middle day must have a small body but this can be of either colour, and may also be a doji. If there are gaps between the shadows of the middle day and the other two (again like our Western island idea) then it is known as an abandoned baby pattern.

As with bar charts, we also look for bigger patterns made up from a series of candles such as head and shoulders, triangles, double bottoms and our rounded bottom (which Japanese a call Fry Pan Bottom).

In conjunction with the formations one uses trend lines, plus support and resistance levels, moving averages and volume, as in conventional technical analysis.

One final thing to note: record sessions. If, in a bull market, prices post new highs on each and every successive day for eight to ten days, the chance of a reversal is strong. Conversely, on the way down, eight or ten successive lower lows are known as record session lows (or Sakata's bones, referring to the man who developed the candles). These are especially reliable if the moves culminate with reversal candles like Dojis. Again, in Western analysis we would become very wary after such a straight line run.

If all this is starting to sound too complicated, do not worry. The main advantage of using candlesticks when charting is that the closing price relative to the open stands out clearly, and spikes or false breaks of a trend line can be easily spotted as these are shadows. With practice, your eyes become able to skim over many charts and pick out quickly those that are interesting and worth watching; the ones showing markets on the move or trends that are reversing.

Figure A-13: Dec gold on COMEX

Charting programs

A list of charting data providers and charting services that offer Ichimoku charts:

- Bloomberg – www.bloomberg.com
- CQG – www.cqg.com
- Reuters – www.reuters.com
- Updata – www.updata.co.uk

My approach to technical analysis

You may be interested to know how I work, so here is some background.

I work in a medium-sized treasury dealing room (about 100 traders), not in an ivory tower. This helps – although at times it can be very noisy – because I can immediately tell when trading volume is high. This is especially hard to gauge in the FX and other over-the-counter markets, such as options and interest rate swaps. The traders also give me ideas as to what is moving and what Joe Average is focusing on at the moment. They constantly seek me out and we discuss trends and strategies and we do a lot of work buying one thing and selling a related but slightly different product. So, a lot of cross-currency trades, say Norwegian krone versus Swedish krona, or Gilts versus Bunds, and so on. From their track records I have learnt that this can be an extremely neat and profitable way to trade.

My daily routine

Every day I grab a coffee and sit down early in the morning (06:00) and look through hundreds of charts: hourly, daily, and weekly ones (the latter only on a Monday); monthly charts on the first day of a new month. Each and every weekday (never at weekends because I am not a masochist) the same sequence of charts. Never deviating from the order in which I open them up. Think of it as being similar to flipping quickly through a magazine that you buy regularly. In fact, in the olden days we did get weekly chart books sent to us and we would grab them asap and flip through the pages.

This is my favourite time of day as it is quiet, I am on my own, and I get totally engrossed in the charts. Why? Because with my lovely little candles, I can quickly pick out what is noise and what has made a significant move over the previous 24 hours.

What am I looking for?

1.   New highs and lows

2.   Massive one-day moves

3.   Major reversal patterns, both on the day and over a longer period of time

4. Patterns that are building or have been completed

Then I draw lines around the patterns and trend lines as necessary. Readjust as appropriate for each time frame.

Note: a weekly trend line must be drawn with weekly candles, a daily one with dailies.

I consider whether data is clean: does it really reflect market activity? Was it a mis-hit? This is especially important to us, because our FX orders circle the globe 24 hours a day. We have to know whether our New York or Tokyo offices were able to fill the order at the price. I am often called in when there are disputes between offices and customers. My charts have to be very clean when millions are at stake.

Watching the herd

While I am doing this I watch a financial TV channel. Headline news is a must – considering whether it may affect any of the markets I cover, directly or indirectly. This is helpful in deciding which markets to spend a little more time on, especially if the chart patterns are already building into something interesting. I make a note of which charts to cover later in the day. But above all, the presenters and guests help me measure what is the prevailing perceived wisdom and consensus forecasts. An invaluable 'guesstimate' for a semi-contrarian like myself. I want to know when the last of the herd has thundered in. This is when you get the truly explosive surprise moves that form the dramatic reversal candlesticks as the herd then tries to squeeze back through what has become a very tiny gate.

Adding the retracements and moving averages

Then I add Fibonacci retracements and projections as required on the charts; dragging these up or down if prices have broken above or below recent ranges. It's worth considering using the less conventional proportions. For example, 75% and 78.6% work well in markets that are moving in broad consolidation phases. Do not be too strict when levels are breached. Relatively small intra-day moves beyond the retracement levels are extremely common, and more often than not constitute some sort of extension or false break. Wait until the end of day and see where the market eventually settles. If it closes within retracement levels, and if this is accompanied by some sort of reversal pattern, it is very likely that prices will hold within the established range. For this reason I also often draw trend lines from the body of the candle rather than from its extremes. Do not be afraid to bend the rules because what you are looking for is where the market really should be – not some sort of blip caused by traders trying to set off stops. Where fair value is currently seen to lie.

Next I add moving averages and other indicators. 10-day, 20-day, 50-day and 200-day simple moving averages. Some markets work well with the first two, and here I give these quite a bit of weight for the medium term trends. 50-day and 200-day moving averages I use because so many other people are aware of these. Not just technical analysts, but a whole host of fund managers and day traders. Why a day trader focuses on these is a mystery to me, but I know they do. Keep one step ahead of the competition, I say.

I don't use indicators much

Indicators in general I hardly use; I call these 'math'.

I can hear it coming already: What! No MACD? No Bollinger? No Chaikin? No envelopes? Heresy! Oh dear, here we go again. Why do I feel I have to justify my methods? I have found that many critics are relatively new to TA – the ones trying to find the philosopher's stone. The ones that are back-testing some truly creative new black box system that will take all the stress out of trading and guarantee humungous profits year after year and they will retire to their yacht and mansion by the age of 35... etc. Oh yeah!

But my main focus is the psychology and feel of the market, and therefore I prefer working as closely as possible to price data - 'raw meat' I like to think of it as. The maths drags you one step or more away from all of this and you no longer smell the greed and the fear.

So which, if any, oscillator-type studies do I use?

The basic ones, once again, to keep up with what others are looking at.

- Fourteen-day **Relative Strength Index**, but only when it is at extremes (i.e. over 70 or below 30).
- **Momentum** and **On Balance Volume**.

- **Volume** and **Open Interest** in markets where that is available. Where it is not, like FX, I keep a close eye on the number of trade tickets generated by our spot desk.

- **Implied volatility** always (note: this is 'raw' and not processed data which is the case of historical volatility).

And that's about it really. As I say, just keep an eye on what others are looking at. My main focus is on the candlesticks, patterns, retracements, trends, and the Clouds.

Elliott Waves

One small thing I do occasionally (keeping quiet about it): Elliott Wave counts. Despite my surname I do not use these often. However, over the years I have been convinced that there is some extremely important value in these. I can feel it instinctively. I have done research with the very long-term trends, using wheat prices from the 1200s and sugar since it was first introduced into Europe. I feel that Elliott Waves have a superior contribution here and I have tried again and again to apply the counts: 1,2,3,4,5 then A,B,C. My success rate: 50:50. Either I must practise a lot harder, or it is not for me - this is nowhere near my usual accuracy rate. I know that many economists are content with correlations of 65% and above. Coming from the more rigorous science of psychology, where you may have to administer mind-bending drugs to schizophrenic patients, correlations of less than 98% are considered irrelevant.

Elliott Waves then. As I say, I can feel it in my bones, yet it doesn't really seem to work despite my best efforts.

- **Long term** – probably; and where it is really useful is in knowing roughly at what point of a very major trend you are. In other words: are you about halfway through, or near the end?
- **Medium term** – I find it useless.
- **Short term** – I find it extremely useful in working out how far periods of consolidation are likely to last and how they will map out. This links in very well with the Wave Principle.

You may have noticed that many Cloud patterns are closely related to Elliott Wave swings. Nevertheless, I tend to keep all of this very quiet. Why? Unfortunately, thanks to the Prophets of Gloom, too many associate this method with alarmist calls and dogma. There is nothing like an Elliott Wave convert to bore me ad infinitum with his (usually) counts and alternative counts.

Rant over.

Clouds with the candlesticks

Finally, I add the Cloud analysis to my candlestick charts. Usually I only look at daily ones, but for important changes in trend I will flick between daily and weekly charts. I note where prices are, relative to the Cloud, and look for reversal patterns, something which is especially important when the two are very close together. I look to see whether the Cloud remains fat for a long time, or whether it becomes very thin in the next week to ten days. I then quickly check the moving averages, but really give these very little weight. More difficult is to untangle Chikou Span. This one so often gets knotted up within the previous candles that it can be hard to see where support and resistance levels for today might lie. If it looks too messy, I tend to ignore this completely.

Conclusion

So, in the end, I am like so many Japanese dealers – who really are only interested in the Clouds themselves. I make no apologies, but having already looked through all the analyses as listed above, I feel entitled to call it a day.

There is of course the risk of overkill, where so many different methods are overlaid that the technical analyst never has a firm opinion. In a funny way, the order in which I still do my analysis is the same one in which I assimilated the tools of my trade. The first things I give more weight to, the last things the least.

Recommendations

Searching for anomalies

The most interesting part of drawing and analysing charts is deciding which pieces stand out as anomalies:

- new recent highs or lows,
- big daily moves,
- the instrument that goes up when all others are trading down.

Also accept when an instrument is going nowhere, and don't dismiss it at once. Some of the most successful dealers are those who like working with markets that are hugging predetermined ranges.

Different asset classes

I also compare different asset classes:

- money markets pricing-in rate hikes way beyond what is realistic, and which could rattle other instruments;
- bond yields below the norm;
- excessive strength of high-yield currencies, especially if the herd has only just latched on.

The reason I am so interested in these is that they often produce the quickest short- and medium-term profit opportunities.

Time frame

Obviously, time frames are important. The spot trader, who wants to make a quick buck out of his order book and a few technical levels, will have little interest in where the Cloud lies in 26 days' time. I work in all time frames: from the next five hours to the next five years (although generally I am very reluctant to predict beyond two years). Charts must be selected that are appropriate to the required time frame.

A picture is worth a hundred words

I like using very big charts relative to the amount of text. If a picture is worth a hundred words, why bother with too many words? In fact, I try to write as little as possible. I don't go in for long descriptive essays of what has happened.

Some analysts write text and trade ideas in a way that they will never be wrong. For example:

> "if we hold above X, then we should rally to Y, but on the other hand..."

Well, yes.

Economists tend to do this a lot. I would rather be wrong than write waffle to cover my backside. Above all, remember that when writing for the professional market as I do, these people have access to thousands of pages of research every day! How many trees do you want to fell, and how much indigestion do you want to cause the reader? Therefore I keep mine as short as humanly possible.

Target market

Finally, I have to think about who the target market is and how they will receive it. The proliferation of media/mail/phone systems has made it easier to be in touch but more difficult to model documents appropriately. I stick to email, website and the Bloomberg terminal – for the moment.

My first set of reports is ready by 07:15am, the time that most of the others start strolling in. This is also in plenty of time for our Tokyo colleagues to read and make use of the analysis. I then go out to get breakfast, after which the cycle starts up again. More slowly now, as I tend to look at the slightly longer term trends and markets that I am not necessarily covering daily.

You may think it all sounds very boring but I love my job and find it fascinating. It's like playing with the most enormous jigsaw puzzle where I know I have all the pieces. The problem is that I don't know the picture into which they will fit. That is what I have to work out and it certainly keeps me on my toes.

Table of sample calculations for FTSE 100

Date	High	Low	Close	Mid-price	Tenkan-sen	Kijun-sen	Senkou Span A	Min(52)	Max(52)	Senkou Span B	Chikou Span
01-Sep-05	5342.1	5296.9	5328.5	5319.5	5285.3	5308.3	5207.5	5022.1	5386.4	5069.1	5372.4
02-Sep-05	5338.1	5319.6	5326.8	5328.9	5289.5	5310.8	5211	5022.1	5386.4	5076.5	5362.3
05-Sep-05	5341.8	5320.6	5337.8	5331.2	5290.6	5313.1	5216.1	5022.1	5386.4	5082.3	5374.5
06-Sep-05	5366.6	5337.8	5359.2	5352.2	5295.7	5315.5	5222.6	5022.1	5386.4	5103.6	5380.7
07-Sep-05	5376.1	5358	5365.9	5367.1	5304.8	5318.4	5231	5022.1	5386.4	5129	5342.2
08-Sep-05	5365.9	5338.4	5340.8	5352.2	5314.8	5320	5240.8	5022.1	5386.4	5143.7	5265.2
09-Sep-05	5362.4	5340.3	5359.3	5351.4	5325.5	5321.2	5251.2	5022.1	5386.4	5144.6	5275
12-Sep-05	5380.7	5359.3	5375.1	5370	5338.9	5323.2	5260.5	5022.1	5386.4	5146.1	5286.5
13-Sep-05	5377.8	5329.3	5338	5353.6	5347.3	5324.4	5268.2	5022.1	5386.4	5149.3	5263.9
14-Sep-05	5349.7	5327.1	5347.4	5338.4	5349.4	5324.6	5275.7	5022.1	5386.4	5154.1	5167.8
15-Sep-05	5387.1	5342.5	5383.5	5364.8	5353.4	5325	5284	5022.1	5387.1	5163.9	5164.1
16-Sep-05	5418.7	5375.3	5407.9	5397	5360.7	5326.1	5292.9	5022.1	5418.7	5175.2	5142.1
19-Sep-05	5435.8	5388.3	5429.7	5412.1	5367.4	5327.8	5300.2	5022.1	5435.8	5175.2	5207.6
20-Sep-05	5446.6	5410.9	5416.4	5428.8	5374.2	5330.5	5308.4	5158.3	5446.6	5181.3	5182.1
21-Sep-05	5416.4	5369.7	5369.7	5393.1	5378.8	5332	5313.8	5180.2	5446.6	5181.3	5227.8
22-Sep-05	5395.5	5354.3	5385.7	5374.9	5381.4	5333.5	5316.7	5180.2	5446.6	5181.3	5182.8
23-Sep-05	5417.4	5383.6	5413.6	5400.5	5384.8	5337.2	5317.2	5180.2	5446.6	5183.4	5213.4
26-Sep-05	5456.9	5413.6	5453.1	5435.3	5393.9	5343	5315.9	5180.2	5456.9	5185.3	5317.3
27-Sep-05	5471.2	5442.7	5447.3	5457	5407	5349.4	5314.1	5180.2	5471.2	5185.3	5344.3
28-Sep-05	5494.8	5447.3	5494.8	5471.1	5418.8	5355.2	5313.9	5180.2	5494.8	5197.8	5358.6
29-Sep-05	5508.4	5467.1	5478.2	5487.8	5428.9	5362.1	5311.8	5180.2	5508.4	5199.9	5431.9
30-Sep-05	5506.1	5462.6	5477.7	5484.4	5437	5369.8	5308.6	5180.2	5508.4	5199.9	5423.6
03-Oct-05	5515	5474.9	5501.5	5495	5444.3	5378.8	5304	5180.2	5515	5199.9	5460.8
04-Oct-05	5501.5	5475.2	5494.4	5488.4	5454.9	5387.7	5299.3	5202.7	5515	5203	5460.9
05-Oct-05	5494.4	5427.8	5427.8	5461.1	5464.5	5395.9	5294.9	5228.1	5515	5204.3	5439.8
06-Oct-05	5427.8	5358.1	5372.4	5393	5463.6	5400.3	5293.8	5228.1	5515	5204.3	5423.5
07-Oct-05	5394.4	5355.7	5362.3	5375.1	5456.9	5402.4	5296.8	5228.1	5515	5204.3	5465.1
10-Oct-05	5395.8	5362.3	5374.5	5379.1	5448.3	5404.4	5300.2	5228.1	5515	5204.3	5470
11-Oct-05	5404.4	5373.9	5380.7	5389.2	5439.2	5406.6	5301.8	5228.1	5515	5204.3	5439.6
12-Oct-05	5380.7	5342.2	5342.2	5361.5	5425.2	5407	5305.6	5228.1	5515	5204.3	5430
13-Oct-05	5342.2	5256.3	5265.2	5299.3	5404.6	5404.4	5311.6	5228.1	5515	5204.3	5460
14-Oct-05	5293.8	5245.6	5275	5269.7	5379.6	5401.2	5317.4	5228.1	5515	5204.3	5498.9
17-Oct-05	5297.1	5272.5	5286.5	5284.8	5356.9	5398.6	5323.4	5228.1	5515	5204.3	5497.9

Date	High	Low	Close	Mid-price	Tenkan-sen	Kijun-sen	Senkou Span A	Min(52)	Max(52)	Senkou Span B	Chikou Span
18-Oct-05	5303.2	5259.6	5263.9	5281.4	5337	5395.2	5331.1	5228.1	5515	5204.3	5517.2
19-Oct-05	5263.9	5167.8	5167.8	5215.9	5317.3	5389.9	5335.8	5167.8	5515	5204.3	5531.7
20-Oct-05	5234	5146.7	5164.1	5190.4	5296.8	5384.2	5337	5146.7	5515	5204.3	5511
21-Oct-05	5164.1	5130.9	5142.1	5147.5	5271.1	5375.9	5339.2	5130.9	5515	5204.6	5523.8
24-Oct-05	5210.1	5140.1	5207.6	5175.1	5247.3	5367.3	5343.4	5130.9	5515	5220.4	5477.4
25-Oct-05	5222.4	5182.1	5182.1	5202.3	5229.6	5359.3	5347.6	5130.9	5515	5229	5491
26-Oct-05	5236.5	5182.1	5227.8	5209.3	5219.6	5350.8	5352.4	5130.9	5515	5302.5	5423.2
27-Oct-05	5227.8	5168.2	5182.8	5198	5211.6	5343.3	5355.4	5130.9	5515	5313.4	5486.1
28-Oct-05	5226.9	5157.6	5213.4	5192.3	5201.3	5336.3	5357.4	5130.9	5515	5313.4	5528.1
31-Oct-05	5318.4	5213.4	5317.3	5265.9	5199.6	5331.1	5361	5130.9	5515	5313.4	5510.4
01-Nov-05	5350.3	5304.9	5344.3	5327.6	5212	5327	5368.4	5130.9	5515	5318.6	5538.8
02-Nov-05	5364.7	5316	5358.6	5340.4	5228.7	5322.5	5378.2	5130.9	5515	5325.7	5528.8
03-Nov-05	5431.9	5358.6	5431.9	5395.3	5256.2	5319.6	5387	5130.9	5515	5337.5	5531.1
04-Nov-05	5446.4	5418	5423.6	5432.2	5284.8	5317.4	5395.5	5130.9	5515	5344.3	5517.4
07-Nov-05	5471	5415.5	5460.8	5443.3	5311.6	5315.9	5403.4	5130.9	5515	5344.3	5501.5
08-Nov-05	5481.7	5451.1	5460.9	5466.4	5340.1	5314.8	5411.5	5130.9	5515	5347.6	5507.2
09-Nov-05	5469.4	5439	5439.8	5454.2	5368.6	5313.4	5421.3	5130.9	5515	5358.9	5521.1
10-Nov-05	5463.9	5423.5	5423.5	5443.7	5396.5	5312.8	5430.2	5130.9	5515	5371.6	5495.3
11-Nov-05	5468.8	5423.5	5465.1	5446.2	5416.6	5314.8	5432	5130.9	5515	5371.6	5531.6
14-Nov-05	5485.9	5455.6	5470	5470.8	5432.5	5318.5	5429.7	5130.9	5515	5371.6	5539.8
15-Nov-05	5470	5424.6	5439.6	5447.3	5444.4	5321.1	5426.3	5130.9	5515	5371.6	5547.9
16-Nov-05	5442.2	5391.7	5430	5417	5446.8	5322.2	5422.9	5130.9	5515	5371.6	5587.4
17-Nov-05	5480.1	5430	5460	5455.1	5449.3	5325.8	5416.1	5130.9	5515	5371.6	5597
18-Nov-05	5531.6	5460	5498.9	5495.8	5455.1	5333.4	5404.5	5130.9	5531.6	5371.6	5595.4
21-Nov-05	5509.4	5486.2	5497.9	5497.8	5458.6	5342.1	5390.4	5130.9	5531.6	5371.6	5622.8
22-Nov-05	5522.4	5497.9	5517.2	5510.2	5464.9	5350.8	5377.8	5130.9	5531.6	5371.6	5638.3
23-Nov-05	5532.7	5507.1	5531.7	5519.9	5473.3	5360	5366.1	5130.9	5532.7	5371.6	5618.8
24-Nov-05	5539	5499.5	5511	5519.3	5481.4	5371.6	5353.6	5130.9	5539	5341.4	0
25-Nov-05	5531.4	5511	5523.8	5521.2	5487	5384.4	5340.5	5130.9	5539	5330.9	0
28-Nov-05	5554.9	5477.4	5477.4	5516.2	5494.7	5398.5	5323.5	5130.9	5554.9	5323	0
29-Nov-05	5507.4	5451.3	5491	5479.4	5501.6	5410.2	5307.3	5130.9	5554.9	5323	0
30-Nov-05	5491	5423.2	5423.2	5457.1	5501.9	5420.1	5294.4	5130.9	5554.9	5323	0

Bibliography

Ichimoku Kinko Studies, Hidenobu Sasaki, Toshi Raider Publishing, 1996
The Japanese dealers' bible.

Beyond Candlesticks, Steve Nison, John Wiley and Sons Inc, 1994
The definitive book on candlestick charting.

Technical Analysis and Stock Market Profits, Richard W. Schabaker, FT/Prentice Hall, 1997
An unbelievably clear book that I urge all aficionados to read.

Technical Analysis of Stock Trends, Edwards and McGee, Amacom Books, 1997
My first and, to date, most inspiring book was *Technical Analysis of the Stock Market* by Edwards and McGee. Support and resistance, based on simple chart patterns and trends, is central.

The reason I like the Schabaker and Edwards and McGee books so much is that underlining their work is the concept of raw emotion: fear and greed. As a social psychologist by training, human motivation has always been especially fascinating to me. So while on first reading you will probably focus on the details of the patterns, when you re-read the texts (and you must at least three times) you will begin to understand that we are looking at a much broader spectrum of generalised human behaviour.

Elliott Wave Principle, Frost and Prechter, New Classics Library, 1990

The W. D. Gann Method of Trading, Gerald Marisch, Windsor Books, Brightwaters NY, 1990

Some books not directly related to the markets

The Great Japan Exhibition, Royal Academy of Arts/Weidenfeld & Nicholson, 1981

Hokusai 36 views of Mount Fuji, Muneshige Narazaki, Kodansha International Ltd, 1968

Painting in the Yamato Style, Saburo Ienaga, Weatherhill/Heibonsha, 1973

Useful references

Nippon Technical Analysts Association: www.ntaa.or.jp

UK Society of Technical Analysts: www.sta-uk.org

International Federation of Technical Analysts: www.ifta.org

Index